WORKING CLASSICS

# WORKING
# CLASSICS

## Poems on Industrial Life

Edited by
*Peter Oresick & Nicholas Coles*

UNIVERSITY OF ILLINOIS PRESS
*Urbana and Chicago*

Illini Books edition, 1990
©1990 by the Board of Trustees of the University of Illinois
The copyright to individual poems remains the property of each
author or original publisher.
Manufactured in the United States of America
1  2  3  4  5  C  P  5  4  3


*This book is printed on acid-free paper.*


Library of Congress Cataloging-in-Publication Data

Working classics : poems on industrial life / edited by Peter Oresick
and Nicholas Coles.
    p.    cm.
    ISBN 0-252-01730-7 (cloth : alk. paper). — ISBN 0-252-06133-0 (paper :
alk. paper)
    1. Working class writings, American.  2. American poetry—20th
century.  3. Working class—Poetry.  4. Industry—Poetry.  5. Work—
Poetry.  I. Oresick, Peter.  II. Coles, Nicholas.
PS591.W65W6  1990
811'.54080355—dc20
                                                        89-20578
                                                        CIP

# CONTENTS

v

vii

ACKNOWLEDGMENTS

JAMES B. ALLEN. "Night Shift at the Plating Division of Keeler Brass" is used by permission of the author.

CATHERINE ANDERSON. "Jonas," reprinted from *In the Mother Tongue* by Catherine Anderson, is used by permission of the author. ©1983 by Catherine Anderson. "Womanhood" first appeared in *The Women's Review of Books* and is used by permission of the author.

MAGGIE ANDERSON. "Among Elms and Maples, Morgantown, West Virginia, August, 1935," "Mining Camp Residents, West Virginia, July, 1935," and "Gray," reprinted from *Cold Comfort* by Maggie Anderson, are used by permission of the University of Pittsburgh Press. ©1986 by Maggie Anderson.

ANTLER. Excerpts from *Factory* are reprinted by permission of City Lights Books. ©1980 by Antler.

RICHARD BLESSING. "Late News" was first published in *Poetry Northwest*.

ROBERT BLY. "Condition of the Working Classes: 1960" is used by permission of the author. "Condition of the Working Classes: 1970," reprinted from *Sleepers Joining Hands* by Robert Bly, is used by permission of Harper & Row, Publishers, Inc. ©1970 by Robert Bly.

DEBORAH BOE. "Factory Work" first appeared in *Poetry* and is used by permission of the editor. ©1986 by The Modern Poetry Association.

JOSEPH BRUCHAC. "Two Pictures of My Grandparents: 1914," reprinted from *Near the Mountains* (1987, White Pine Press), is used by permission of the author.

DAVID BUDBILL. "Old Man Pike" and "Bobbie" are reprinted from *The Chain Saw Dance* by David Budbill. "Roy McInnes" is reprinted from *From Down to the Village* by David Budbill. All poems are used by permission of the author.

LORNA DEE CERVANTES. "Cannery Town in August," reprinted from *Emplumada* by Lorna Dee Cervantes, is used by permission of the

University of Pittsburgh Press. ©1981 by Lorna Dee Cervantes.

DAVID CITINO. "Visiting My Father in Florida," first published in *The Minnesota Review,* is used by permission of the author.

MARY JOAN COLEMAN. "Golden Gloves: Beckley, West Virginia," reprinted from *Take One Blood Red Rose,* is used by permission of West End Press. ©1978 by Mary Joan Coleman.

BRENDA CONNOR-BEY. "Martha" is used by permission of the author.

VICTOR CONTOSKI. "Galena, Kansas" first appeared in *Raccoon* and is included in *A Kansas Sequence* by Victor Contoski, ©1983, published by Cottonwood/Tellus.

JIM DANIELS. "4th of July in the Factory" is reprinted from *On the Line* (1981, Signpost) by Jim Daniels. Used by permission of the author. All other poems are from *Places/Everyone* by Jim Daniels, ©1985, published by the University of Wisconsin Press. Used by permission of the publisher.

KATE DANIELS. "Self-Portrait with Politics," reprinted from *The White Wave* by Kate Daniels, is used by permission of the University of Pittsburgh Press. ©1984 by Kate Daniels.

JAMES DEN BOER. "Father Finds a Job in America," reprinted from *Learning the Way* by James Den Boer, is used by permission of the University of Pittsburgh Press. ©1968 by the University of Pittsburgh Press.

PATRICIA DOBLER. All poems are reprinted from *Talking to Strangers* by Patricia Dobler, ©1986, published by the University of Wisconsin Press. Used by permission of the publisher.

STEPHEN DUNN. "Hard Work," reprinted from *Work and Love,* is used by permission of Carnegie Mellon University Press. ©1981 by Stephen Dunn.

HARLEY ELLIOTT. "Numbers" first appeared in *The Expatriate Review.* Used by permission of the author.

MARY FELL. "The Triangle Fire" originally appeared as a limited edition chapbook by Shadow Press, U.S.A., ©1983. "In Coal" first appeared in *Quindaro.* "Not Working" first appeared in *West End.* These poems and "Picket Line in Autumn" and "Out-of-Luck, Massachusetts" are reprinted from *The Persistence of Memory,* published by Random House, ©1984. Used by permission of the author.

*Minnesota Review*. All other poems are from *Definitions* by Peter Oresick (1990, West End Press). ©1990 by Peter Oresick.

GREG PAPE. "A Job on the Night Shift," reprinted from *Black Branches* by Greg Pape, is used by permission of the University of Pittsburgh Press. ©1984 by Greg Pape.

JAY PARINI. "Anthracite Country," reprinted from *Anthracite Country* (Random House, 1982), was first published in *Poetry* in 1976. "Coal Train," "Working the Face," "The Miner's Wake," and "Playing in the Mines," reprinted from *Anthracite Country*, are used by permission of Random House. ©1982 by Jay Parini.

KENNETH PATCHEN. "The Orange Bears" is reprinted from *Collected Poems* by Kenneth Patchen. ©1949 by New Directions Publishing Corp.

DONALD A. PETESCH. "On the Line in Oakland, California" was first published in *Poetry Northwest*.

ANTHONY PETROSKY. All poems, reprinted from *Jurgis Petraskas* by Anthony Petrosky, are used by permission of Louisiana State University Press. ©1983 by Anthony Petrosky. "A Pennsylvania Family" and "Photograph" originally appeared in *Ironwood*.

KEVIN RIPPIN. Both poems are from a work-in-progress, "Belle's Body," and are used by permission of the author.

DAVID RIVARD. "Torque," reprinted from *Torque* by David Rivard, is used by permission of the University of Pittsburgh Press. ©1988 by David Rivard. "Strangers" is used by permission of the author.

LEN ROBERTS. "Coal Miners" and "At the Train Tracks" are reprinted from *Sweet Ones* (1988, Milkweed Editions). ©1988 by Len Roberts.

CAROLYN M. RODGERS. "Aunt Dolly" is used by permission of the author.

LIZ ROSENBERG. "Alone with the Shoe Manufacturer in His Memorial Park," reprinted from *The Fire Music* by Liz Rosenberg, is used by permission of the University of Pittsburgh Press. ©1986 by Liz Rosenberg.

VERN RUTSALA. "The Furniture Factory" is reprinted from *Walking Home from the Icehouse,* published by Carnegie Mellon University Press. ©1981 by Vern Rutsala.

by permission of Wesleyan University Press. ©1971 by James Wright. "Honey," reprinted from *This Journey* by James Wright, is used by permission of Random House Publishers. ©1982 by Anne Wright. "Beautiful Ohio," reprinted from *To a Blossoming Pear Tree* by James Wright, is used by permission of Farrar, Straus and Giroux. ©1977 by James Wright.

ROBERT WRIGLEY. All poems, reprinted from *The Sinking of Clay City* (1979, Copper Canyon Press), are used by permission of the author.

We are grateful to many for their contributions to the making of this book. We thank Richard L. Wentworth, director and editor of the University of Illinois Press, who was quick to see the merits of this poetry and was the first to offer us a publication contract. Stephanie Flom was the driving force in the long and tedious permissions process, and she was a helpful and discerning reader of page proofs. Kathleen Plummer assisted with permissions. Terry Sears's careful copyediting of the manuscript prompted many improvements. Finally, we thank the poets. They account for the existence of this book and its virtues, and we appreciate their cooperation and generosity in allowing us to reprint their work.

The poems collected here are about blue-collar America at work—in coal mines, canneries, steel mills, refineries; in glass factories, printshops, sweatshops, lumber mills; making trucks, tires, dresses, ice cream; bottling Coke, cutting paper, packing eggs, cleaning fish. There are also poems about not working—layoffs, shutdowns, strikes, and retirement—and, most important, about the workers themselves, men and women, on the job and off, and their spouses and families and the problems they confront each day.

This is, we know, an unusual kind of poetry, largely absent from the standard poetry anthologies and introductions to literature used in most classrooms. In these textbooks, love, death, and nature appear as the proper subjects for "literature." If work appears there at all, it is usually somebody else's work, observed from a distance, as in the pastoral landscapes of classical oil painting. Yet in a nation such as the United States, where for the last century so much human effort has been devoted to industrial production, it is to be expected that a blue-collar poetry should have developed, one with its own distinctive concerns and voices and points of view. The contemporary work poems in this anthology are direct, energetic, sometimes disturbing, often witty. They offer a way of viewing our experience of industrial society which is at once intimate and public, integrating personal experience into a broader sense of how the world works and changes. Together, they illuminate our history, for the world of these poems is where many of us are from, in both senses of that phrase.

Whether we want it there or not, for most of us work takes up its position at the center of our lives. What we do for a living organizes our time, consumes our energy, and to a large extent determines our experience in every other activity of living. If we are out of work, the lack of it and the search for it take the place of work as the dominant condition. If we are too young to work, our parents' jobs, their work history, affect where and how we live, in what kinds of neighborhoods and with what kinds of prospects. We agree with poet Tom Wayman when he writes that "any literature which omits this governing experience of daily life is a literature with an enormous hole in the middle of it." Our aim with this collection is to reinsert work among the subjects of the American Literature an educated reader could be expected to know, and thereby demonstrate, in Wayman's words, how a person's "attitudes to love and death and nature are in large part shaped by the kind of daily work he or she does."[1]

Any anthology must have parameters. Our primary reason for focusing on industrial work poems, to the exclusion of poems about office work or health care work, for example, is that the industrial way of life we grew up with is rapidly changing—some would say disintegrating—and our instinct is to gather these poems as literary witness to those changes. In making our selection, we reluctantly drew the line at about 1945, working forward from the postwar years to the present. From the whole range of contemporary American poetry, we chose what we felt were the best and most representative pieces on industrial work and its contexts. The result is a collection of 169 poems by 74 poets, nearly a third of them women. Together, these poems offer a unique and graphic record of contemporary industrial America and the changes it is undergoing—changes that, in turn, have contributed to the emergence of work and working-class life as major themes in recent poetry.

We are living through a transformation of the traditional industrial economy into the high tech and service economies that fuel the ongoing civic renaissances in many of our major cities. While glittering corporate towers rise downtown, streets crumble and stores are boarded up in the mill towns and working-class neighborhoods adjacent to those cities. Beginning in the 1970s, in one industry after another—auto, steel, tire, apparel, textile, and electronics—new economic circumstances to which management failed to respond effectively resulted in declining market shares and profits. According to labor analyst John P. Hoerr, these circumstances included: wild fluctuations in world oil markets; the industrialization of low-wage nations such as South Korea, Taiwan, Brazil, and Mexico; relatively high U.S. labor costs; automation; and the fading of American technological supremacy. "Perhaps," he wrote, "the most significant development was the growth of a new technology—based on the silicon chip, microelectonics and the computer—which enables capital . . . to fly about the world on electronic air waves and create new assets in the twinkling of a second."[2] Corporations used this mobility to gain concessions not only from organized labor but from regions within the United States, often pitting the Northeast against the Southwest and inner cities against suburban developments. The result for blue-collar workers, especially in the Rust Belt, has been a period of steep decline marked by unemployment and underemployment due to relocated plants, shutdowns, and capital disinvestment in older plants and industries.

Many of the poems gathered here read like elegies to a way of living and working that is seen to be slipping into the past: to towns that were loved because they were where you belonged, hated because they were also where you were stuck; to mines and mills that gave life but only at the price of taking it; to fathers who sacrificed their family lives in order to support their families. The impulse to remember, to celebrate, to curse that way of life is strong in many of these poems. So too is the impulse to register a sense of continuity in working-class life, a sense of what does not change, at least in its essentials. While it seems likely that by the year 2000 fully half of the American labor force will be working with something called "information," a smaller but significant number of workers will still be getting up each morning and going to jobs like those described here.

Another central impulse in these poems, whether elegiac or focused on the present, is to question the value of the work we find ourselves doing, its social usefulness, its effects on us as people. Sometimes work is seen here as trivializing, as an enforced absorption in minor details; it makes you forget what's important. As the poet Antler puts it: "your only responsibility toward mankind / is to check for defects in the ends of cans" ("Factory"). At other times, in other poems, there is a sense of authentic possibility in work, a pride in having produced something, in doing what few others can do, like the miner in Jay Parini's "Working the Face":

> He was prince of darkness,
> stalking the village at 6 P.M.,
> having been to the end of it,
> core and pith
> of the world's rock belly.

More often, though, what we experience is the ache and waste of exploitation, the sense of energy used up in jobs too small for people: "I never wanted this skill," writes C. G. Hanzlicek, "I wanted a life" ("Machinist").

In these poems the processes of work, and their costs and possibilities, are set within the larger context of "a life" among other lives: in the networks of family and community, for example, or in the relations between men and women, or in the rhythms and stages of working life. We encounter people growing up in mill towns, playing in mine shafts, doing summer jobs, looking for work, going to work, getting home from work, drinking after work, getting laid off, going on vacation, walking the picket line, playing with their children, looking at old photographs, planning, fighting, dreaming, retiring, moving to Florida.

The many poems about fathers pull a number of these experiences into focus; often they speak of loved men whose energies were lost to work through "the need to change life into wages." And yet, repeatedly, even in poems about work's domination of family and community, there is the image of something beyond the working life, something bright that stands out against the shadows of mine or mill. It might be "some abstraction" about changing the world, as in Anthony Petrosky's poem "Jurgis Petraskas, the Workers' Angel, Organizes the First Miners' Strike in Exeter, Pennsylvania." Or it might be some other less definable possibility, as in Tess Gallagher's "Black Money," when the father sets out at dawn for the mill, a certain swagger in his step:

> In a fan of light beyond him
> the Kino Maru pulls out for Seattle,
> some black star climbing
> the deep globe of his eye.

Other poems allow us to see also what life is like in "the tumbled rooms" the working fathers leave behind them at home. The differences between the women's work world and the men's are explored in poems like Joyce Carol Oates's "Women Whose Lives Are Food, Men Whose Lives Are Money" and in this one, titled "Lessons," by Patricia Dobler:

> Aunt Julie's hands knot and whiten
> as she squeezes cucumber slices
> handful by small handful
> into the pale green bowl.
>
> Called away from the uncles
> to help in her hot kitchen,
> I am beginning to learn
> the woman's part. The man's part
>
> is no better. After his mill shift
> Uncle Vernon will stand at the back door,
> shaky and black. He likes
>
> cucumber salad, so this is the least
> Aunt Julie can do: wringing the slices
> as if they are somebody's neck.

A third theme—if we take the value of work itself and its effects on life outside work as two large themes—is the stance of the writer in relation to work: the question of who is writing these poems, from what points of view, and for what purposes. Most of the poets represented here are professional writers, each with a distinguished record of publication. While they are mostly from working-class backgrounds, and while most have done the kinds of work they write about, the majority now work primarily at writing and, in many cases, at teaching that craft to others. In this they differ from most of the worker-writers included in Tom Wayman's pioneering collections of "poetry-on-the-job" that have appeared in Canada: *A Government Job at Last* and *Going for Coffee*.[3] All of those poems, in Wayman's words, "are written from inside the experiences that are described. That is they are written by men and women who have done and are doing the jobs they write about."⁴ The poems collected here have a special interest for us, as writers and teachers who have done these kinds of jobs and grown up around them, in that they are written from a variety of stances, not only inside but outside and alongside the working experiences described.

There are poems, for instance, in which manual work is regarded by an observer as something from which to be rescued. In "The Gentle Weight Lifter" David Ignatow writes of the laborer lifting cement barrels:

> He is fixed in his form,
> save a hand reach from outside
> to pick him up bodily and place him,
> still making the movements that insure his love,
> amidst wonders not yet arrived.

Perhaps the saving hand is the poet's. And in David Wagoner's "Valedictory to Standard Oil of Indiana," former high school classmates, now in the grip of the refineries, are offered some advice:

> As the Laureate of the Class of '44—which doesn't know it has one—
> I offer this poem, not from hustings or barricades
> . . .
> But from another way out, . . .
> . . .
> . . . Get out of town.

The poet feels his own difference from the worker, his privilege to understand and transcend the trap of the jobs that have closed around relatives and friends. So too does Kate Daniels write of "a world that gave me / poetry and my brother an assembly line": "I mourn the loss of all I think / he could have been," his exclusion from "the life / of the mind I have chosen to live" ("Self-Portrait with Politics").

A similar stance is made explicit in the poems that reflect the experience of working summer jobs while in college. Stephen Dunn, in "Hard Work," exercises "the prerogatives of [his] class" by quitting the job,

> . . . though someone for sure
> still does the hard work of boredom
> and that person can't escape,
> goes there each morning
> and comes home each night
> and probably has no opportunity
> to say who he is.

In other poems the writer works these jobs specifically in order to be in a position to understand them, to be able to say who the worker is, "to do for Continental Can Company / what Walt Whitman did for America," as Antler puts it in "Factory." The poet tells himself, " 'If I don't work here / this poem won't be able to write me.' " He represents one form of the movement to the inside, a movement in which "poetry" and "assembly line" need not inhabit separate cultural spaces but can inform and interpret each other.

This movement has antecedents, as Antler suggests, in the poetry of Walt Whitman, who, with his characteristic American vision, set out to democratize poetry, that traditionally elitist, European art. Whitman testified to the beauty and strangeness of all the ways we have to make a living, through his celebration of physical labor, his appreciation of machines and the tools of trade, and his insider's understanding of the soldier's work. His faith in the promise of health and growth through work reads oddly in postindustrial America, yet there is something profoundly modern in his point of view: the stance in which he is both witness to and participant in the common life and all its daily details. Whitman's inheritance, although ignored by academic mentors of the Free Verse movement, nevertheless broadened the sense of poetic possibilities for other writers: Carl Sandburg did for Chicago and William Carlos Williams did for Paterson what Whitman had done for "America."

It is the legacy of Williams, more than any other poet of this century, that we see continued in many of the contemporary work poems in this collection. The poetic values of T. S. Eliot and the high Modernist mode dominated American poetry until the 1950s; as an academic poetry, requiring a professional criticism for its transmission, it seemed removed from the concerns of everyday life. Younger poets in the 1950s, notably the Beat poets, found an alternative model in Williams's concrete and energetic poetry written in a distinctly American idiom. Williams advocated a poetry whose source was in "local conditions" rather than in the traditions of Europe or of classical mythology. This dictum, to write about what one knows firsthand and in language that is direct and idiomatic, had a tremendous influence on subsequent schools of American poetry—the Beats, the Confessional poets, the New York school, and others. It is not surprising, given these antecedents, that so many American poets should produce poems illuminating some of their most local conditions—the conditions of workplaces and of the men, women, and machines working in them. In the majority of poems gathered here, "the life of the mind" goes to work on work itself, the raw material of everyday life: describing its processes, naming its tools, recording its special languages, capturing its rhythms of sound and movement, celebrating the small victories of escape, sabotage, or even genuine production.

Sometimes, though not nearly often enough, working, like writing, can mean producing something useful and beautiful. The title of Edward Lahey's poem about building a mine tunnel, "Contributor's Note," has a nice double meaning: his contribution as a laborer, his contribution as a poet. Working, at its best, and writing, also at its best, are acts of creative transformation: earth becomes glass, steel becomes truck cabs, hours become wages, the line becomes music, the factory becomes a jungle, miracles become commodities—just as in James Wright's "Beautiful Ohio" the sewage of Martins Ferry becomes the material for poetry. He could also be writing about work.

> I know what we call it
> Most of the time.
> But I have my own song for it,
> And sometimes, even today,
> I call it beauty.

To end on this note, though, is to leave a false impression. In most of these poems, work is "what we call it / most of the time," and the object of the writing is not necessarily beauty. These poems typically do not aestheticize labor or an industrial way of life. Rather, they offer, in the way good poems do, an experience of that life through which we can explore the meanings of work in our own lives: what we get out of work, what work takes out of us, how work got to be this way, and how it might be different.

NOTES

1. Tom Wayman, *Inside Job: Essays on the New Work Writing* (Madiera Park, B.C.: Harbour, 1981), p. 12.

2. John P. Hoerr, *And the Wolf Finally Came: The Decline of the American Steel Industry* (Pittsburgh: University of Pittsburgh Press, 1988), p. 24.

3. Tom Wayman, ed., *A Government Job at Last: An Anthology of Working Poems, Mainly Canadian* (Vancouver, B.C.: MacLeod, 1975); *Going for Coffee: An Anthology of Contemporary North American Working Poems* (Madiera Park, B.C.: Harbour, 1981).

4. Wayman, "Introduction," *Going for Coffee,* p. ix.

Instead of grouping poems by subject or era, we have chosen simply to arrange the collection alphabetically by author. However, we have provided a subject index to help readers locate poems about particular themes or types of work. Poems on themes discussed in the Introduction, for instance, would be listed under such headings as "pride in work," "men and women," "fathers," and "writing about work." (For obvious reasons the largest categories, such as "work," "industry," and "factory," have been omitted.) We hope in this way to accommodate readers who may be using the anthology in the context of, for example, urban studies, history, sociology, or women's studies courses, and who may require a selection of poems on, say, unemployment, sex and work, or the steel industry.

*Working Classics*

JAMES B. ALLEN

## Night Shift at the Plating Division of Keeler Brass

The secretaries drive by the factory
Dreaming of rich uncles.
Across the street at Charley's,
The bar is jammed.
The neon sign pops and blinks
Like a wounded eye.
The heat rises over Godfrey Street.
In the plating section at Keeler Brass,
The acid bubbles in the iron tanks.
I strip down to my shorts,
Pull on the rubber gloves,
And lift heavy racks into the tanks,
The tendons in my arms
Pulse at the wrists.
Old Dutch works beside me,
An Allegan farmer,
He milks twenty-five cows
Before he comes to work.
He knows that college kids are worthless,
And works to wear me down.
In the last aisle, he swings the brass
Before a giant fan, the sweat drying
On his face as the metal drips
And shines like gold.
He moves among the vats,
Dreaming of metallic women in wheatfields,
Humming like machines.
He glows like burnished metal.
I am tempted to push him in,
A huge brass-plated skeleton
Swinging before the fan.
Instead, I soap my acid burns in the shower,
And hit the street, deserted now
Except for an indian walking his dog.

1

## *Jonas*

We were threshing envelope after white envelope
on a conveyor in redundant Detroit,
your sons bought you twenty-four Dutch Masters,

Jonas Raimundas

one hangs from your lip like a bitten sausage.
It is amazing how your mouth moves around it;
you are speaking Lithuanian to the gears,
and to me you are saying again
how they first shot your mother and then your father.
You rolled their muslin wrapped bodies to the sea
because it was January;
you were fifteen,
your shoulders could not break the earth,
and now, at night, you believe
the Baltic is rising over there while
you are here.
Your uncles have always said
you have dark hair,
the color of your mother's,
and eyes, too,
as blue, as deep as ikons.

## Womanhood

She slides over
the hot upholstery
of her mother's car,
this schoolgirl of fifteen
who loves humming & swaying
with the radio.
Her entry into womanhood
will be like all the other girls'—
a cigarette and a joke,
as she strides up with the rest
to a brick factory
where she'll sew rag rugs
from textile strips of kelly green,
bright red, aqua.

When she enters,
and the millgate closes,
final as a slap,
there'll be silence.
She'll see fifteen high windows
cemented over to cut out light.
Inside, a constant, deafening noise
and warm air smelling of oil,
the shifts continuing on . . .
All day she'll guide cloth along a line
of whirring needles, her arms & shoulders
rocking back & forth
with the machines—
200 porch size rugs behind her
before she can stop
to reach up, like her mother,
and pick the lint
out of her hair.

3

## Among Elms and Maples, Morgantown, West Virginia, August, 1935

Houses are wedged between the tall stacks
of Seneca Glass beside the Monongahela
and waffle up steep hills. Here, the terrain
allows photographers to appear acrobatic.
Walker Evans liked standing on a hill, focusing
down so it seemed he was poised on a branch.
He liked the single telephone pole against
the flat sky, crossed off-center like a crucifix.
Beneath it, among elms and maples, is the house
my mother lived in with her sister and their mother
nearly fifty years ago. In this shot, Evans
only wanted the rough surfaces of clapboard
houses, their meshed roofs and slanted gables.
He didn't want my mother peeling the thin skin
from tomatoes with a sharp knife, my clumsy
Aunt Grace chasing the ones she'd dropped
around the linoleum floor. That would be another
picture, not this one. I look back from the future,
past the undulating, unremitting line of hills
Evans framed my family in, through the shaggy fronds
of summer ferns he used as foreground and as border.

*Mining Camp Residents, West Virginia, July, 1935*

They had to seize something in the face of the camera.
The woman's hand touches her throat as if feeling
for a necklace that isn't there. The man buries one hand
in his overall pocket, loops the other through a strap,
and the child twirls a strand of her hair as she hunkers
in the dirt at their feet. Maybe Evans asked them to stand
in that little group in the doorway, a perfect triangle
of people in the morning sun. Perhaps he asked them
to hold their arms that way, or bend their heads. It was
his composition after all. And they did what he said.

# *Gray*

Driving through the Monongahela Valley in winter
is like driving through the gray matter
of someone not too bright but conscientious,
a hard-working undergraduate who barely passes.
Everybody knows how hard he tries. I'm driving up
into gray mountains and there, it may be snowing
gray, little flecks like pigeon feathers, or what
used to sift down onto the now abandoned slag piles,
like what seems to sift across the faces
of the jobless in the gray afternoons.

At Johnstown I stop, look down the straight line
of the Incline, closed for repairs, to the gray heart
of the steel mills with For Sale signs on them. Behind me,
is the last street of disease-free Dutch elms in America,
below me, a city rebuilt three times after flood.
Gray is a lesson in the poise of affliction. Disaster
by disaster, we learn insouciance, begin to wear
colors bright as the red and yellow sashes on
elephants, whose gray hides cover, like this sky,
an enormity none of us can fathom, though we try.

EXCERPTS FROM
*Factory*


II


"All you have to do is stand here
        and package lids as they come from the press
        checking for defects every so often.
Shove enough lids in the bag like this,
Stand the filled bag on end like this,
Fold over the top like this,
Pull enough tape off
        and tape it like this,
Then stack 'em like this on the skid."


How many watching me watch the woman
        teach me my job
Remembered *their* first day on the job,
Remembered wondering what the woman felt
        teaching them in a minute
        the work she'd done all her life,
Showing them so fast all they needed to know?
How many could still remember who they were in search of a living—
Name, address, telephone, age, sex, race,
Single, married, children, parents, what they do or why they died,
Health record, police record, military record, social security #,
        how far in school, everywhere worked, why quit or fired,
        everything written here is true, signature, interview,
        the long wait, the call "you're hired"—
Could still see themselves led through the factory
        to the spot they would work on,
        strange then and now so familiar?


This is the hall big as a football field.
Here are the 24 presses chewing can lids
        from hand-fed sheets of aluminum.
Here are the 10 minsters chomping poptops

nonstop into lids scooped into their jaws.
Machines large as locomotives,
      louder than loudest rockgroup explosions,
Screeching so loud you go deaf without earplugs,
      where the only way to speak is to gesture,
Or bending to your ear as if I were telling a secret
      the yell from my cupped hands less than a whisper.

Now the film of myself each day on the job begins.
I see myself enter the factory, led to the spot I will work on.
I see myself adjusting the earplugs to stopper the deluge of sound.
I see the woman who showed me the job
      she'd done her whole life in a minute
Let me take over, and the minute she left how I fumbled,
      how the lids gushed all over the floor
And when the foreman rushed over and I hollered—
      "Something's wrong! It's too fast!
      No one can work at this speed!"
How he stared and the stares of the others
      who couldn't hear what I said but could tell.
And I gulped, This "Beat the Clock" stunt
      must be performed *eight hours*
      before the lunatic buzzer itself
      becomes consolation prize.

Yet sooner than I thought, I mastered the rhythms,
      turned myself into a flywheel dervish,
And can't deny being thrilled by the breakthrough
      from clumsy to graceful—
Though old-timers scowled as if it took years
      to learn all the fine points.
But long after my pride in doing such a good job
      turned into days crossed off the calendar
      each night before pulling out the alarm
         I woke to push in,
      up, eat, go, work, eat, work, back, eat, sleep,

All the days I would work stared
        ahead of me the line of machines,
        behind me the line of machines,
Each with a worker working as I work,
        doing the same job that I do,
Working within sight of the wall clock
        whose second hand is still moving.


## III


Thus as the foreman watched me from the corner of his eye
        as I watched him from the corner of mine
        pretending to be doing my best
                as if I didn't know I was under inspection,
I relished the words I would write
        intoned in this factory where no one could hear them,
        swallowed in the shrill-greased ecstasy of machines
                as I led processions of naked acolytes
        sopranoing Athenian epitaphs, candles in their hands.

To write this poem, to bring the word beautiful into Factory
You must never forget when the lids first come from the press
        they are hot, they are almost slippery.
You must never forget since each tube holds 350 lids
        and each crate holds 20 tubes and each day I fill 40 crates
From my work alone 280,000 lids each day—
        huge aluminum worm wriggling one mile long
        into the cadaver of America.
You must never forget 14 million cans each day
        from a single factory!
5,110,000,000 cans each year from a single factory!
More throwaway cans each year than human beings on this planet!
Every high, every heartbeat of your life
        the machines have been running.
Every time you heard a pianissimo

9

the earsplitting machines have been running.
You've already spent more time working here
    than making love,
More time working here than lying on hills
    looking at the sky.
Each of your favorite books you must pilgrimage here to age,
    to absorb and exude wisdom,
To think of those who worked here before you
    and those who will work here after you.
You must say to yourself—"If I don't work here
    this poem won't be able to write me."
And asked—"What's that smell?" you must remember
    on your clothes, on your skin, in your lungs
    and when the breeze is just right through your bedroom window
        the smell of the factory.
You must brainstorm machines and workers are like poets and readers:
    the poets eat sheets of steel and press them into words
        that are the ends of containers,
The reader stands in one place shifting from foot to foot,
    crating and crating,
Searching for defects so the noisemaker can be shut down
    and while white-coated mechanics scurry to fix it
    like doctors around a sick president, he can take a break,
        get a drink, take a crap, unwrap some butterscotch to suck on,
            glimpse a glimpse of second-shift sunset,
            watch the guard lower the flag.

To birth this womb, to do for Continental Can Company
    what Walt Whitman did for America,
You must celebrate machine-shop rendezvous!
You must loafe observing a disc of aluminum!
You must sing the security of treadmills
    remembering where you are today
    you were yesterday
    you will be tomorrow.
So, after suicide invites you through the naked mirror

10

and poetry dares you to dive headfirst into the sky,
After memorizing the discovery of fire, tools, speech,
    agriculture, industry,
And all the inventors, inventions and dates
    of the last 10,000 years you got a 100 on in History,
And after the ceaseless history of human war
    reads the eyes in your face,
Faced with the obituary of man,
Caught in the deathrattle of the world,
    from the deathblows of pollution,
    from the deathknells of overpopulation,
    from factories which are the deathbeds of Nature
        and the seedbeds of bombs,
After contemplating the graveyard of elegies,
    the immortality of maggots
    and the immolation of the sun,
Then, Antler, or whatever your name is,
Enjoy returning prodigal to your machine
    to forget the view from the skyscrapers of money,
    to forget the hosts of human starvations
        belly-bloated or brainwashed in Mammon,
    to forget the sign over the entrance to Auschwitz
        WORK MAKES MAN FREE,
    to forget that working here you accomplice
        the murder of Earth,
    to forget the birds that sing eight hours a day
        daydreaming the salaries of worms,
    to forget how old you must be
        to be rich and young before you die,
    to forget your mother waking you
        from this nightmare
        is only a dream—
So nothing called life can torment you with undertakings
    and your only responsibility toward mankind
        is to check for defects in the ends of cans.

## X

O thinking so much makes me weary.
Maybe I should pretend the masters
Nodding their heads in the invisible auditorium
        in which continual dialogues are held
        on the progress of my computerized soul
                are only a dream.
Maybe if I just stop thinking and look at the machines—
        the way the lids pour out like suicide battalions,
        the way I pretend to check for defects every so often,
        the way I shove enough in the bag like this,
        the way I stand the filled bag on end like this,
        the way I fold over the top and tape it like this,
        the way the rows of 'em rise on the skid like this—
MMMMMM, that's better, now I'm myself again—
All I have to do is stand here
        and package factories as they come from the press—
Factories that make cans.
Factories that make the machines that make cans.
Factories that make the machines that make the machines
        that make cans.
Factories that make factories.
Factories that make factories that make factories
        that make everything that goes into cans.
Factories that make canopeners.
Factories that make electric canopeners.
Factories that make candy and canoes.
Factories that make candles and candelabras
        and incandescent lightbulbs.
Factories that make cuckoo-clock canaries.
Industries of canned laughter, canned applause,
        canned music.
Telephone factories, television factories,
        radio, stereo, tape recorder factories,
        refrigerator, stove and toilet factories.

Telescope factories, microscope factories,
      film, camera, movie screen factories,
      jukebox, roulette wheel and slot machine factories.
Industries of nuts! Industries of bolts!
Industries of bulldozers, roadgraders, steamshovels,
      cement mixers, steamrollers, jackhammers,
      pile drivers and wrecking cranes!
Every building and street in every dot on the map
      and all the highways between them
      constructed from products of multitudinous factories!
Factories of cars and toy cars,
      trucks and toy trucks, trains and toy trains,
      planes and toy planes, ships and toy ships,
      spaceships and toy spaceships!
Factories of money and factories of play money!
Factories of all that money can buy!
Mass production of pricetags!
Assembly lines of cash registers!
Application and paycheck form factories!
Lunchbucket and thermosbottle factories!
Earplug and timeclock and alarmclock factories!
      and self-winding watches given factoryhands at retirement
      made in what factories!
Factories of lady's ware, men's ware, children's ware, baby's ware,
      silverware, copperware, tinware, glassware,
      stoneware, woodenware, earthenware, plasticware,
      furniture, souvenirs, knicknacks, novelties,
      gizmos, geegaws, glockenspiels and greeting cards!
Ambulances, police cars and buses from factories!
Fire engines, fire escapes and matches from factories!
Sirens, foghorns, steamwhistles, rockguitars, grandpianos,
      every instrument in the orchestra including the baton
      and the concert hall all hatched from myriad factories!
O every record I love I know where you come from!
O cookiecutters! birdhouses! buddhastatues and plastic vomit!
      I know where you come from!

O awls, axes, adzes, augers,
Barrels, bearings, bellows, brads,
Crowbars, corkscrews, crucibles, calipers,
Dumbbells, dollies, dibbles, drills,
Exhausts, excelsior, forceps, faucets,
Gauges, gouges, gaskets, goggles,
Hammers, hammocks, hangers, hoists,
Irons, icepicks, jewels, jacks,
Keels, kilns, levels, ladles, lathes,
Mops, muzzles, mattresses, microphones,
Nails, neon, napalm, ouija boards,
Pistons, pitchforks, pliers, puncheons,
Quivers, quoits, ratchets, rounces,
Radar, roachclips, scales, scalpels,
Snorkels, stencils, shovels, shoetrees,
Squeegees, tweezers, trophies, trocars,
Tampons, trampolines, uniforms, umbrellas,
Vises, valves, wormgears, wrenches,
Wigs, wire, yardsticks, zippers—
I know where you come from!
And I know where the machines that make you come from!
And all the letters for alphabet soup!
Breweries, canneries, tanneries, creameries,
(Name me something not come from Factory)
Brassworks, gasworks, refineries, binderies,
Plants that make barberpoles, barberchairs,
        dentistchairs, electric chairs,
        electric knives, electric fans,
        electric shavers, electric blenders,
        electric blankets, electric fireplaces,
        electric toothbrushes, electric eyes!
*Everything in the Sears Roebuck Catalogue*
        *is not from the legendary herds of buffalo!*
Typewriter sweatshops! Motorcycle sweatshops!
Revolving door sweatshops! Intercom sweatshops!
Mass production of straightjackets!

Mass production of bombs!
Vast spectrum of death machines of land, sea and sky!
More bullets than people who ever lived!
More bayonets than books ever written!
Better machines for killing invented so fast
        they're obsolete before used!
So much an hour mass production of crosses and flags!
Purple-heart gristmills! Basket-case gristmills!
Industries of homicidal deceit:
        glamorizing cigarets no different than Nazis
        telling Jews gas chambers are shower rooms!
Millions of new cradles and coffins each year!
Corpses rolling down the conveyor belt of the funeral factory!
Slaughterhouse factories and all the machines of the slaughterhouse:
        cleavers, bludgeons, meat-hooks, sticklers!
Fish, mammal, bird factories! Fruit, vegetable, grain factories!
        Every bite processed in factories!
Strip me naked, abandon me in deepest woods in Canada—
        my body still from Factory!
My flesh flesh of what factories raised from birth
        and murdered for my mouth!
Supermarket Factories! University Factories!
Hospital Factories! Prison Factories!
        Death Factories!
Stop! Don't you think I get the point?
All the floors of the department store
        and the elevator girl telling me
                the goods on each as the doors open?
Is it necessary to list
        every machine necessary to extract raw materials
        and every machine necessary to transport them
        and every machine necessary to transform them
                into iron, steel, aluminum,
        and everything made from iron, steel, aluminum,
        and every machine necessary to make it?
What do I get for unveiling the machinery that makes

15

footballs, baseballs, basketballs, tennisballs,
bowlingballs, billiardballs, pingpongballs, snowmobiles,
boxinggloves, golfclubs, sailboats, surfboards,
scubagear, bathtubs and easychairs?
Must we see the slaves behind every device of recreation and leisure?
Must we see the slaves behind every laborsaving device?
(Do you think it's trite to call them slaves?
Are you only a company man or Literature
slaving on the disassembly line of criticism?
Are you only a cog in the Poetry Factory?
How many poems by Zinjanthropus
appear in your Immortal Anthology?)
Wheelbarrow factories! Kitchen sink capitalisms!
Staplegun generalissimos! Toothpick presidents!
Paperclip czars! Linoleum pharaohs!
Punchpress emperors! Pushbutton potentates!
Monopoly millionaires! Deodorant billionaires!
Electricity trillionaires! Computer quadrillionaires!
Quintillionaires of wood! Sextillionaires of rock!
Septillionaires of plastic! Octillionaires of oil!
Nonillionaires of flesh! Decillionaires of Oblivion!
The exact number of pennies ever made!
The exact number of papercups ever made!
The exact number of number two pencils ever made!
More rope! More tape! More pipe! More fence!
More wallets! More purses! More needles! More thread!
More envelopes! More stamps! More brushes! More paint!
More boxes! More bottles! More screws! More screwdrivers!
More washingmachines! More airconditioners! More vacuum cleaners!
More flashlight batteries!
Dynamos stretching to the horizon and still not enough!
More generators! More blastfurnaces! More concrete! More antennae!
Capitalisms of thumbtacks and thumbscrews!
Stockholders in tongue-depressors and rectal thermometers!
Manufacturers of lawnmowers, snowblowers, toenail clippers
and machetes!

World's largest producers of arrows, slingshots, fishhooks,
    riflesights, decoys, traps, and raccoon death-cry calls!
Peddlers of pills and more pills and pill containers
    and prescription forms!
Industries for the Blind! Industries for the Retarded!
Where artificial flavor and color are made!
Where artificial flowers and grass are made!
Where artificial eyes and arms and legs are made!
    and wherever they make boobytraps!
    and wherever they make tiddlywinks!
    and wherever they make doors and doorknobs
        and doorbells and hinges and locks and keys!
Corporations of bulletproof vests and silencers!
Corporations of blowtorches, rivetguns and girders!
(And where do dildoes and bathyspheres fit in?)
Every breath more parkingmeters and bankvaults
    and armored trucks and turnstiles
    and wedding rings and vagina dolls
    and rubbers and rubberbands
    and rubber rafts and lifepreservers
    and thingamabobs and thingamadoodles
    and gargle and garbage trucks
        and garbage cans
        and sprinkling cans
        and aerosol cans
        and "Eat" signs
        and "Stop" signs
        and "No Trespassing" signs
    and switchboards and turbines
    and conveyor belts of conveyor belts!
And the world's largest producers of machineguns and chainsaws!
And 20,000 a day extermination factory of Auschwitz!
And one billion gallons of gasoline burned in California each month!
And 38 cigarets inhaled every day in New York City
    just by breathing the air!
And even you, backpacks, compasses, and maps of the wild?

must you be from factories?
*Et tu* mountain climbing gear?
And even icecream and kaleidoscopes
    and bubblewands and balloons
        and swingsets and teetertotters
        and yoyos and marbles
        and frisbees and skateboards
        and pinwheels and merrygorounds
        and beanies with propellers
        and the hall of mirrors?
Must we see the slaves behind every toy of our childhood?
Must we see the gypped lives behind the pantheon of laughs?
    O souls flophoused by factories!
    O geniuses imbeciled by factories!
    O enlightenment shoplifted by factories!
Copying machine factories! Calculating machine factories!
Vending machine factories! Change machine factories!
Humans spending their lives making lipstick or eyeshadow!
Humans spending their lives making crystal balls or fortune cookies!
Humans spending their lives making calendars or blindman canes!
Working your way up to foreman in the insecticide factory!
Working your way up to employment manager in the squirtgun factory!
Working your way up to the top in the pay toilet factory!
    40 years making piggybanks!
480 months making burglar alarms or handcuffs!
2,000 weeks making wind chimes, wind machines
    or wind-up toys!
10,400 days of your life
    making stopwatches or metronomes!
83,200 hours of your life
    making miniature replicas of Rodin's Thinker!
4,992,000 minutes of your life
    gluing the hemispheres of globes together!
299,952,000 seconds of your life
    cranking out the links of chains!

## Late News

In a small town in western Pennsylvania, a Polish workman
is killing everyone.

            Who can say how the world seems
to Dombrowski this morning? It is as different
as a doberman's or a general's.

                If this is a war,
Dombrowski is winning. If we are the enemy,
as by now we are, cover his hairy chest with ribbons.

Dombrowski peers out of his shell of a house
and the neighbors go round like neighbors
in a gallery and the police go round.

A man down the line at the plant says *Things
ate on him lately, but no more than nobody else*.
He does not wish to be named.

            The dead
do not wish to be named, pending notification.

It is a quiet neighborhood, the kids lying
beside their bicycles, the lovers kissing nothing
forever on the porch swing.

            Is there something
Dombrowski wants? The chief says *A nut like that,
they ought to kill themself*.

                What if, in sullen wisdom,
we give in, retreat from the little town, or all
of Pennsylvania? Let the mad inherit their corner
of earth.

        There would be space for miles

where only wind would blow. After a while, the mines
would go back to the grass. Bass would lie deep
in the Allegheny, as if they had never gone away.

One morning even Dombrowski might lay down his gun,
walk naked in a meadow that had been his yard.
Great waves of butterflies would ride the wind
and the ground would drum with distant hooves.

There is a sun so old no man has seen it.
In Pennsylvania, Dombrowski lifts his eyes.

## Condition of the Working Classes: 1960

There are bricks trapped in thousands of pale homes,
And pale children who in time will vote Republican,
Who sleep at night with black stones beneath their
      pillows;
I have seen cars ascending into the heavens,
Where their fenders turn slowly to drifting clouds;
Driving down the streets, we see the faces of
      children
Change suddenly into the doors of aircraft factories,
That are far off the street, behind grass, with a blue
      door;
And the doors change at night into small holes in
      paper
Behind which the blue sky is seen; and the sky
      changes to decks of cards
Thrown down on a cardtable at midnight, and locked
      away in boxes,
And the paper boxes change to chunks of pine
      standing beneath axles
In lazy garages where the wooden floors are stained
      with oil,
And the extricated axles change to missiles with
      warheads
Climbing up, and the stages change into aisles
      of a church,
And the church-doors change into the faces of
      children standing beside the new trees.

## Condition of the Working Classes: 1970

You United States, frightened by dreams of Guatemala,
building houses with eight-mile-long wings to imprison the Cubans,
eating a bread made of the sound of sunken buffalo bones,
drinking water turned dark by the shadow of Negroes.
You remember things seen when you were still able to speak—
white wings lying in a field.
And when you try to pass a bill,
long boards fly up, suddenly,
in Nevada,
in ghost towns.

You wave your insubstantial food timidly in the damp air.
You long to return to the shell.
Even at the start Chicago was a place where the cobblestones
got up and flew around at night,
and anarchists fainted as they read *The Decline and Fall*.
The ground is soaked with water they used to boil dogs.

Your sons dream they have been lost in kinky hair,
no one can find them,
neighbors walk shoulder to shoulder for three days,
but your sons are lost in the immense forest.

And the harsh deer drop,
the businessmen climb into their F-4s,
the chocks are knocked out,
the F-4 shoots off the deck,
            trailing smoke,
dipping slightly,
            as if haunted by the center of the ocean,
then pulling up again, as Locke said it would.

Our spirit is inside the baseball rising into the light

So the crippled ships go out into the deep,
sexual orchids fly out to meet the rain,

22

                the singer sings from deep in his chest,
memory stops,
                        black threads string out in the wind,
the eyes of the nation go blind.

The building across the street suddenly explodes,
wild horses run through the long hair on the ground floor.
Cripple Creek's survivors peer out from an upper-story window, blood
        pours from their ears,
the Sioux dead sleep all night in the rain troughs on the Treasury
        Building.

The moonlight crouches over the teen-ager's body thrown from a car

The weeping child like a fish thrown from the herring block
the black-nosed Avenger leaping off the deck

Women who hear the cry of small animals in their furs
and drive their cars at a hundred miles an hour into trees

## Factory Work

All day I stand here, like this,
over the hot-glue machine,
not too close to the wheel
that brings up the glue,
and I take those metal shanks,
slide the backs of them in glue
and make them lie down
on the shoe-bottoms, before the sole
goes on. It's simple, but the lasts
weigh, give you big arms.
If I hit my boyfriend now,
in the supermarket parking lot,
he knows I hit him.

Phyllis, who stands next to me,
had long hair before the glue machine
got it. My machine ate up my shirt once.
I tried to get it out, the wheel
spinning on me, until someone with a brain
turned it off. It's not bad
here, people leave you alone,
don't ask you what you're thinking.

It's a good thing, too, because all this morning
I was remembering last night,
when I really thought my grandpa's soul
had moved into the apartment,
the way the eggs fell, and the lamp
broke, like someone was trying
to communicate to me, and he
just dead this week. I wouldn't
blame him. That man in the next aisle
reminds me of him, a little.

It's late October now, and Eastland
needs to lay some people off.

Last week they ran a contest
to see which shankers shanked fastest.
I'm not embarrassed to say
I beat them all. It's all
in economy of motion, all the moves
on automatic.
I almost
don't need to look at what
I'm doing. I'm thinking of the way
the leaves turn red when the cold
gets near them. They fall until
you're wading in red leaves up to your knees,
and the air snaps
in the tree-knuckles, and you begin
to see your breath rise
out of you like your own ghost
each morning you come here.

## Two Pictures of My Grandparents: 1914

### I.

Her feet stitch the sidewalks
of the Garment District.
It is as grey
in those distant stories
as the shawls
of Middle European women.

Her fingers are thin,
polished bone spools.

### II.

The sun peers down on him
through coal-smoke clouds.
It squints like the Asian eye
of a Slovak steelworker.

His breath is hesitant
from burned lungs.
It whitens the throat
of the winter sky.

### III.

My Uncles do not recognize
their parents in these words.
The images are as strange to them
as that language they still remember
is to me, a tongue

which never gathered money
though it warmed them
as they shared it, the one fire
they could always afford.

## Old Man Pike

Old man Pike was a sawyer at the mill
over in Craftsbury.
He lived just down the road from here.
Every morning he walked six miles through the woods
over Dunn Hill saddle while the sun rose.
He took dinner and supper in the village
then walked home across the mountain in the dark.
Sally Tatro who used to live on my place
would hear him coming through the night, singing.
Sometimes he'd stop to gossip
but mostly she only saw him stride by the window
and disappear.

The old man could have stayed at home,
milked cows, like everybody else,
but he needed an excuse to go and come
through the mountains, every day,
all his life, alone.

Old man Pike didn't believe in the local religion of work,
but out of deference, to his neighbors maybe,
he bowed to it,
placed its dullness at the center of his life,
but he was always sure, because of his excuse,
to wrap it at the edges of his days
in the dark and solitary amblings of his pleasure.

## Bobbie

For years Bobbie drove the pickup truck to Morrisville
every day to sew the flys in men's pajamas at a factory
down there. When you spoke to her about the job,
she'd blush and turn on her heel like a little girl.
She was good. The best one down there.
It was piecework and she was fast.
She quit the sewing when she and Doug went to farming.

Bobbie is beautiful, or could be.
Under thirty years of work and plainness you can see
her body, see her face,
those definite, delicate features
glowing.
She strides like a doe.
In spite of two brown teeth
her smile is warm and liquid.

Last summer she cut off a finger in the baler,
paid her farmer's dues.

Now she holds her missing finger behind her when she talks.
She's got something new to blush for.

*Roy McInnes*

## The Man

Roy McInnes is a welder. He spends his life
with chains and block and tackle, steel and torches,
lives his days inside a hood looking like
a medieval warrior, peering through a small rectangle
of blackened glass, watching light brighter than the sun.
He listens to the groan of generators, the crack and snap
of an electric arc liquefying steel. His hands
are always dark and on his upper lip there is
a mustache
as if wiped there by a greasy finger.

Roy McInnes is a small man and frail.
He speaks quietly and slowly and moves that way.
He seems at ease inside his body, comfortable there.
When you shake his hand his grip is warm and gentle
and you can feel the calm he carries in his person
flow into your arm.

Roy and I were visiting one day, years ago,
after we had got to know each other some,
and we got to talking about work
and I said, because I was afraid to tell the truth,
that I'd just about rather garden than do anything,
to which Roy responded, and there seemed to be
some sadness in his voice,
"Well, I don't know about just about.
All I know is what I'd rather do than anything.

I'd rather weld."

## The Truck

Roy's truck is an extension of himself,
which is not to be confused with the way some people
buy a fancy car with velour seats, electric windows
and suddenly start wearing cardigans and oxfords, suddenly become
little more than yet another piece of optional equipment.
In Roy's life it is the truck that gets transformed.

I met his truck the day I first met him.
Not that he introduced me or anything like that,
it's just you can't help noticing.

When Roy bought the truck new-to-him, it was just a pickup,
a common insect like a million others identical to it.
He brought it home, put it in his shop and six weeks later
it emerged a strange, metallic butterfly, unique and fanciful,
translated to
an articulation of his private vision,
a function of Roy's need and whimsy.

New, the truck was rated at three-quarter ton,
but with the added braces to the frame, heavier shocks,
special springs, dual rear wheels and heavy duty tires
it can carry four.

Roy cut the bed away right down to the frame
and welded on a diamond-plate floor and roof,
using two inch steel pipe for posts, one at each four corners,
one in the middle on each side. Then up forward,
toward the cab and half-way back, he welded
sheet metal walls and welded shelves to them
and all the shelves have doors on hinges, all made of steel.
There are hooks and clamps welded to the walls everywhere
so when he goes down a bumpy road his tools won't bounce around.

31

Roy McInnes is a carpenter who builds with steel,
with boiler plate and torches.
In place of nails he binds his dream
with hydrogen and oxyacetylene.

Shaper, moulder, alchemist,
intermediary, priest,
his hands communicate a vision,
they create with skill and grace
an act of intercession between reality and need.


### The Shop: Part I

Roy's house and shop are on the edge of town.
The shop was built in stages.
The tall center section with its steep-pitched roof
is sided with slabs from the local mill, whereas
the lean-to shed on the left
is particle board; the one on the right is Homasote.

Summer people say it's ugly, but what they can't, or won't,
understand is: the sidings write a history
of its construction. Rome wasn't built in a day either.

When Roy built the center section he needed an opening
large enough to admit big trucks, like loggers' rigs,
but couldn't afford the kind of rising, jointed,
overhead doors gas stations and garages have
so he found a way to use ordinary storm doors,

the kind with glass so he could get some light in there,
by hitching them with hinges side to side
and stacking them three high so that now he's got
two folding doors which make an opening fifteen feet wide
and seventeen feet high: two doors of doors
made from eighteen smaller doors.

Roy heats the shop with a homemade, quadruple-chamber,
oil-drum stove: four fifty-five gallon drums:
two side by side above one, the fire box, and one above the two:
a glowing diamond of cylinders all welded to each other
and held apart by rods and all connected by a pipe
which leads the smoke from one drum to another and finally,
when it has bled the smoke of heat, exits to the chimney.

Beyond the stove at the back of the shop
stacked willy-nilly against the wall
there is an intricate confusion of iron pipes, cast iron scraps,
angle iron, sheets of aluminum and steel, diamond plate,
expanded metal, loops of heavy wire and braided cable
and a half-dozen categories of other things I can't identify—
a mine, the raw material of his dreams.

The shop is always cluttered, dirty and there is
a permanent grime that clings to everything.
Generators and tanks of gas and orange rubber hoses
snaked across the floor. The place smells of oil and grease,
of that molecular rearrangement of the air the welder's arc
produces.

This is a place where—against the grinder's scream and whine,
the moan of generators straining, the crackling spit of metal
rent asunder—human speech is pointless, drowned

in a cacophony of unearthly voices. And when the machines
get still, it is a place to see through the smoky fog
something medieval, brooding, dark, fantastical.

It would be so easy to see this place as sinister,
to see the wizard/priest who rules this lair as evil,
that would be so easy if
you didn't know that he is Roy—
the one who lets the calm of his body flow into your arm
when you touch his hand.


## The Shop: Part II

Stand in the highway; look at the shop straight on;
pretend it isn't what it is; get beyond its function.
Look at its lines, at the proportions of height to width,
sheds to center section—an early Christian basilica,
or something Gothic.

The tall center section, narrow, steep-roofed—the nave.
The sheds—the aisles,
roofed over flying buttresses.
And those doors of doors are cathedral doors.

There are no rose windows here, no clerestory, no triforium,
no vaulted ceilings or clustered piers, and it's ratty,
but it soars—not too high or very gracefully
but it soars.

It is a January day.
The doors of doors fold open.
Roy appears in hood and grimy apron.

Then, just down the road, smoking through the village,
the penitent comes, the one who seeks the healing touch
of fire.

Guy Desjardins, trucker of logs and lumber
who just this morning while loading the biggest butt-log beech
he ever saw in his life, snapped the boom.
The truck lurches down the road, clam and boom dangling,
a wounded beast, Gargantua's broken arm. Guy shifts down,
pulls to the doors of doors and in.

There are no acolytes, no choir
but the engine sings its cracked and pulsing song
and the censer spurts heady clouds of smoke to the rafters.

The doors come closed, truck shuts down
and for a moment Guy and Roy stand
before the diamond juggernaut of cylinders, their hands
outstretched in ritualistic adulation, a prelude to the mass.
The boom is jacked and steadied, readied for the altar
of cutting flame: The Mass of Steel and Fire.

From the clutter of his accidental reredos
Roy brings angle iron. A ball peen hammer bangs,
generator moans, light arcs and snaps, steel flows
a second time—a liquid, balm, metallic salve
and the healing touch.

When the clanging mass is finished, when the groans
and snaps and spits have ceased, when there is silence,
when only a spiritous wisp of greasy smoke ascends
toward the blue-foggy rafters, when Guy stands
knowing it is done, the celebrant lifts his hood
and says benediction:
"That ought to hold it, Guy."

They drink coffee from dirty cups,
eat doughnuts with greasy hands.
Then Guy backs out, is gone, smoking down the road,
back to the job, leaning on his horn and waving
in what has got to be plain-song, a canticle,
praise and joy for the man,
a chorus of Hallelujahs,
for the reconciling arc of fire.

## Cannery Town in August

All night it humps the air.
Speechless, the steam rises
from the cannery columns. I hear
the night bird rave about work
or lunch, or sing the swing shift
home. I listen, while bodyless
uniforms and spinach specked shoes
drift in monochrome down the dark
moon-possessed streets. Women
who smell of whiskey and tomatoes,
peach fuzz reddening their lips and eyes—
I imagine them not speaking, dumbed
by the can's clamor and drop
to the trucks that wait, grunting
in their headlights below.
They spotlight those who walk
like a dream, with no one
waiting in the shadows
to palm them back to living.

## Visiting My Father in Florida

Forty years, every working day he drove
through the roiling haze of Cleveland streets
to the Harshaw Chemical Co., past Union Carbide,
Rockwell International, Bethlehem Steel, all the
barbed-wire, bricked-windowed plants, sulfur
rising from their stacks to rain on playgrounds
and reservoirs, the states downwind. He knew

the neighborhoods of Italians and Poles, Greeks
and Slovenes, Slovaks and Croats before they moved
their kitchen tables, photo albums and ceramic jockeys
to the suburbs. He couldn't understand the girls
in platform heels and slit skirts who'd whisper
"Hey Mister" from bleak doorways. "Go home to
your mother," he told one once. "Your white ass,"

she answered. He persisted so long even he changed.
Now we drive through his new "planned community,"
banks and K Marts garish as modern churches,
acres of offices of oncologists, proctologists,
urologists, ancient women pedaling tricycles,
Lincoln and Cadillac dealers, the old in bunches
raising blouses and shirts to show their latest scars.

Later we fish his new canal. Caloosahatchee mullet
leap stiffly toward the sky. He lifts his rod
and a whiskered, flat-headed catfish the color
of sludge lands between us, writhing. I've never
seen a thing so old, so ugly. It leaves a trail
of slime on the new dock, lost in so much sudden light,
blind. Its mouth gulps the precious, useless air.

*Golden Gloves*
*Beckley, West Virginia*

girls in fist tight jeans
    with mandolin string voices ringside
   their eyes dance with the moist legs
      of the elderberry cheeked boy
        with blue ribbon eyes
      and mustard flower yellow curls
   scattered damp across his forehead
his Pentacostal mother, her hair in a grey net,
      rubs fear and pride between her palms
  his father, in plaid short sleeves,
   who stamps and boos
     calling punches in a voice
    sharp edged as a power saw;
  a smiling miner in a Big Cat cap
  leans forward to catch blows
the blond boxer staggers and balances
      muhammed from the mountains
   grinding the hard shell prophesies
     of our coal dark years
under his stubborn muscles tonight.

# Martha

from oral history series

when i came to new york
used to work at a factory on twenty-second street
i just prayed for a job
i looked up and
there was a sign in the window saying:

GIRLS NEEDED

that was my signal things would be okay
you know, my mamma taught us to hand embroider
crochet, knit and do fine handwork
that's how we made money at home

i learned big machines at that factory
that sew faster than my eyes could blink
(i tell you) place your foot down
that machine shake your whole body
loose if you ain't attached too good

the man i married was big
you see me small and tiny like this
you ask if i don't mind him so big
(you know what i mean?)
but he tell me he like little women
something about bone and skin
him and strength
lord that man was crazy and had
me loving what momma said was wrong
but he could make the nighttime
music happen in the day

one day i bending over the machine
and I get a catch here between my legs
a tight grippin sensation in my back

40

(i tell you) i stopped that machine
went to the hospital/lost the baby
i ain't even know i carried
my boss wanted to know when
i'd be back to work
(said i worked real good!)

and that big husband of mine
the day i come in from the hospital
dragging my tired bone weary self
(you know i was weak)
he picked me up
carried me to our room
telling me we don't need no children
all we need was this ting here and
we made love so sweet and he
tell me he miss me very much

but look at this ting here now
retire from job
big husband dead thirty years now
they say i can't do nothing
too old
they tell me to relax
enjoy myself
(chips)
i show them my hands
see? my blood still good
why don't you bring me some clothes
you need mending?

# Galena, Kansas

## I.

Deep underground lead
and red zinc crystals
whispered: *money, money.*

On Red Hot Street
women with the same message.

## II.

Galena "the city
that Jack built"

Empire City "a dead man
for breakfast every morning"

fought for business
like men over a woman.

## III.

Now over the radio country singers
whine of careless love and Jesus.

The lead is gone,
the zinc is gone,
Empire City gone.

And Galena hesitates

like someone on an errand
who has forgotten what it was.

## 4th of July in the Factory

Today there is no trouble
finding a parking spot.
There is no line
at the time clocks.

I walk down toward my department
past the deserted, motionless
assembly line in department 65,
past the dark cafeteria.

There is a doubleheader
at Tiger Stadium today.
Someone shouts the score of the first game
and I can hear him.

The foreman smiles
at the thought of all the money he will make today.
I smile with him.

The big press breaks down
after 20 minutes.
We all sit down and tell jokes,
waiting for the foreman to come by and notice.

Bobbie Joe brought in a bottle
and we pass it around.
Even K.Y. the hi-lo driver
gets off his seat
for the first time in recent history
and takes a hit.

When the foreman shows up
we tell him we need an electrician.
A half hour later
some guy with a flashlight
and a belt of tools

strolls toward us rubbing his eyes.
Another half hour goes by
before he gets the press fixed
with the foreman standing over him.
Then, we work until first break.

When we get back
someone wedges in a steel blank the wrong way.
Old Green, press repairman,
motions thumbs down
and walks away.

The foreman threatens to send us home
but instead
sends us on an early lunch.

We go outside to eat,
sitting on huge rolls of steel
and watching the sun set.
We talk about how wonderful it is
to make 20 dollars an hour
for sitting on our asses,
how wonderful it is
to hear voices
when the press is down.

Suddenly Old Green, who cannot speak,
lights up a joint
and takes a hit,
his wrinkled stone face
breaking into a smile
that today
could stop any machine.

*Factory Love*

Machine, I come to you 800 times a day
like a crazy monkey lover:
in and out, in and out, in and out.

And you, you hardly ever break down,
such clean welds, such sturdy parts.
Oh how I love to oil your tips.

Machine, please come home with me tonight.
I'll scrub off all the stains on your name,
grease and graffiti.

I'm tired of being your part-time lover.
Let me carry you off
into the night on a hi-lo.

That guy on midnights,
I know he drinks,
and beats you.

## Factory Jungle

Right after the seven o'clock break
the ropes start shining down,
thin light through the factory windows,
the sun on its way to the time clock.
My veins fill with welding flux—
I get that itchy feeling I don't belong here.

I stand behind the biggest press in the plant
waiting for the parts to drop down into the rack,
thinking about what that mad elephant
could do to a hand.

I'd like to climb one of those ropes of light
swing around the plant
between presses, welders, assembly lines
past the man working the overhead crane
everyone looking up, swearing off booze, pills,
whatever they think made them see me.
I'd shed my boots, coveralls, safety glasses, ear plugs,
and fly out the plant gate
past the guard post
and into the last hour of twilight.

The parts are backing up
but I don't care
I rip open my coveralls and pound my chest
trying to raise my voice
above the roar of the machines
yelling louder than Tarzan ever had to.

## After Work

On this night of blue moon and damp grass
I lie bare-backed on the ground
and hum a children's song.
The air is cool for this, the midnight of July.
The grass pins my sticky back.

You, moon, I bet you could
fill my cheeks with wet snow
make me forget I ever touched steel
make me forget even
that you
look like a headlight
moving toward me.

## Digger Goes on Vacation

The maps from AAA, the tourbooks,
you are well-prepared:
*Florida here we come.*
For the first time
your son will not go with you.
He has a legitimate excuse:
a job at the corner store.
It is only you and the girls.
You think of your wife
as a girl.
You think
that you have given her nothing.
At the first Stuckey's on the road
you buy her a box of peanut brittle
and smile weakly
as she kisses your cheek.
Then you think of the plant
she is kissing you good-bye
in the morning.
You feel a chill
maybe wind on your neck.
You have two weeks.
Your body shakes
as you pull back on the road:
you have fifteen more years.

•

First night
you stop at a motel
off of I-75 in Kentucky.
At a diner
you eat a late dinner
the girls nodding off to sleep
in their hamburgers.
You look at your wife.
If somehow she could lose some weight.
Then you look at your belly

hanging over your belt:
*but mine's hard*, you tell yourself,
*muscle.*

You punch your gut:
*if we could just lose*
*all this weight.*

"Digger?"
"Oh . . . yeah."
You pay the bill
and walk across the street
to the motel
squeezing your wife's hand
like a snowball
you want to melt.

•

You lie in the sand
the sun crisp on your back.
You will get burned.
You always do.
You try to read a book
in the bright glare—
the same book you brought
on vacation last year:
*The Godfather.*
At a cabin in Northern Michigan
you read 150 pages
and killed mosquitoes.
*She packed it to keep me busy,*
*keep my eyes off the women.*

You look over at your wife
wearing a floppy sun hat and bulging out
from her bathing suit.
You throw sand on her belly:

49

"hey Loretta, gimme a beer."
She hands you one
from the cooler by her side.

*She really does*
*care about me,*
you think, and suddenly
you are happy and smile.
You put the cold beer
against her neck
and she jumps up screaming.
"Hey baby, I love you."
"What?"
She takes off her sunglasses
and smiles, hugging you.
"You haven't said that since . . .
last year's vacation!"

You stare out at the sea of skin
and wonder when
you'll say it again.
•
At the beach
your foot in the sand
outlines the part
you weld onto axles.
"What's that, Daddy?"
You kick sand
over the drawing,
"Nothin'."
But no matter how many times
you kick the sand
it still looks like
something.

•

In a motel in Tennessee
you peel off your skin
to gross your daughters out.
"Oh Daddy, that's sick!"
You laugh
and rub your vacation beard:
"when all this skin is gone
I'll be a new person."
"Who will you be then, Daddy?"
"I'll be an astronaut.
So I could get lost in space."
"You're already lost in space,"
your wife shouts from the bathroom.

That night after dinner
you drink alone
at a local bar.
Your hands hold up your head
like obedient stilts.
This is how you always
become a new person.
You talk to the bartender:
"I used to be an astronaut."
And he believes you.

## Hard Times in the Motor City

When Louie got married
somebody gave him
a broken bicycle for a present
in all sad seriousness.

Louie gave it back—
him and his new wife
traveling light—
a toaster and clock radio
heading south west east
wherever jobs might be.

•

Up and down the streets
men mow their lawns
do yardwork
many try to grow vegetables.

Some of the wives work now
behind counters at McDonald's
marking clothes at K-Mart
pulling in minimum wage
grocery money for another week.

Everybody's already had a garage sale.

•

In the bar
Steve talks about
the afternoon tv movie
about Elvis
about fighting
anyone.
He says he'll dig ditches
or clean shitholes
all he wants is a job.
He's got a wife, two kids.

He looks me hard in the eye:
"A man can always afford a drink."

&bull;

Dennis, laid-off trucker
borrowed some money
took his rig to Florida
loaded up a truck full of pot
sells it out of his basement
to help make house payments.

Dennis sits on his porch
smoking up the profits
singing old rock and roll songs
his electric guitar plugged into the bushes.

&bull;

An old man talks about the Great Depression:
"You don't see nobody jumpin' out of windows
around here."

But in the backyards of Detroit
Warren, Hazel Park, Center Line
men on their knees
pray over
their rotten tomatoes
their deformed carrots
their ragged, ragged lettuce.

## Still Lives in Detroit:
## #2, Parking Lot, Ford Sterling Plant

Empty pallets stacked against the fence,
a few cars scattered across the blacktop,
a barren landscape decaying under grey sky.

*167 days since the last work-loss accident*
*This lot under closed circuit surveillance*
*Authorized personnel only*

An empty bag blown flush against the fence.
A set of keys in the middle of an aisle.
A flattened oil can, a lottery ticket,
a paperback with no cover.

There's a man in this picture.
No one can find him.

## Self-Portrait with Politics

At the dinner table, my brother says something
Republican he knows I will hate.
He has said it only for me, hoping
I will rise to the argument as I usually do
so he can call me "communist"
and accuse me of terrible things—not loving
the family, hating the country, unsatisfied
with my life. I feel my fingers tighten
on my fork and ask for more creamed potatoes
to give me time to think.

He's right: It's true I am not satisfied
with life. Each time I come home
my brother hates me more for the life
of the mind I have chosen to live.
He works in a factory and can never understand
why I am paid a salary for teaching poetry
just as I can never understand his factory job
where everyone loves or hates the boss like god.
He was so intelligent as a child
his teachers were scared of him.
He did everything well and fast
and then shot rubberbands at the girls' legs
and metal lunchboxes lined up neatly beneath the desks.
Since then, something happened I don't know about.
Now he drives a forklift every day.
He moves things in boxes from one place
to another place. I have never worked
in a factory and can only imagine
the tedium, the thousand escapes
the bright mind must make.

But tonight I will not fight again.
I just nod and swallow and in spite

of everything remember my brother as a child.
When I was six and he was five, I taught him everything
I learned in school each day while we waited for dinner.
I remember his face—smiling always,
the round, brown eyes, and how his lower lip
seemed always wet and ready to kiss.
I remember for a long time his goal in life
was to be a dog, how we were forced
to scratch his head, the pathetic sound
of his human bark. Now he glowers
and acts like a tyrant and cannot eat
and thinks I think
I am superior to him.

The others ignore him as they usually do:
My mother with her bristly hair.
My father just wanting to get back to the TV.
My husband rolling his eyes in a warning at me.

It has taken a long time to get a politics
I can live with in a world that gave me
poetry and my brother an assembly line.
I accept my brother for what he is
and believe in the beauty of work
but also know the reality of waste,
the good minds ground down through circumstance
and loss. I mourn the loss of all I think
he could have been, and this is what he feels,
I guess, and cannot face and hates me
for reminding him of what is gone and wasted
and won't come back.

For once, it's too sad to know all this.
So I give my brother back his responsibility

or blandly blame it all on sociology,
and imagine sadly how it could have been different,
how it will be different for the son I'll bear.
And how I hope in thirty years he'll touch
his sister as they touched as children
and let nothing come between the blood they share.

## Father Finds a Job in America

Following his father, to this land and work,
my father limps through more than thirty years

at his long work; he welds himself with
hands in flames, his face dark-masked.

Noon whistles, and he eats alone each day,
chewing his loneliness for bread and meat,

brushing away flies, waxed paper at his feet.
Through dusty windows where he stands,

ignites and melts his steel, America
stretches across its famous fields and hills

farther than his light-scarred and weakened
eyes can see. All he sees are pheasants

pecking for seeds of grasses blown down
among the rusting twisted scrap-heaps

by what he believes is wind beginning
in the sea he never saw. He enters

the heavy mask, and his children swim
up to meet him in that green sea-light;

those he fathered in this land of flames
that burn his seed to loneliness like steel.

## Steel Poem, 1912

for Kevin

When the mill crept into his bunkroom
beating a fist on his wall

and the sun rose in sulphur
piercing the company house

he dressed with the men
cursing the lard on his bread

the sponge of new steel
waiting for him and his brothers

the shovel and pound
the steel rolling out

and he dreamed of dovehunting
plump birds hanging like fruit

the soft bones eaten with flesh
how that tempered the heart of the eater.

## My Father's Story, 1932

The blast furnaces dead, the cities dark,
the iron and ice ringing underfoot
but ringing for nothing, all for nothing,
no light in any house but kerosene,
the Depression a huge fact, a frozen hump
he couldn't get over or around,
the primitive helplessness
of his parents—outraged,
the young man leaves to cut
ice on the pond, 40¢ an hour,
his bucksaw biting deep
into another man's property.
If he can't shape steel
he will sheathe these blocks
in yellow sawdust and lay them up
against the coming heat.
The ice at least will have
its occupation: in July, sweating
his sweat, oozing golden drops
onto the ice house floor.

# The Mill in Winter, 1939

Below them, the valley cradles
the mill's dark body which lay
for a decade like a stunned animal,
but now awakes, almost innocent again
in the morning light. A pale disk of sun
pinks the crusted snow the men walk on,
the first thin columns of smoke brush the sky,
and the sharp odors of coke and pickling acid
drift toward them. They taste metal on their tongues
and yearn toward the mill's black heart.
To enter, to shut out the bright cold air
is to enter a woman's body, beautiful
as ashes of roses, a russet jewel,
a hot breath grazing their arms and necks.

## Field Trip to the Rolling Mill, 1950

Sister Monica has her hands full
timing the climb to the catwalk
so the fourth-graders are lined up
before the next heat is tapped, "and no
giggling no jostling, you monkeys!
So close to the edge!" She passes out
sourballs for bribes, not liking
the smile on the foreman's face,
the way he pulls at his cap,
he's not Catholic. Protestant madness,
these field trips, this hanging from catwalks
suspended over an open hearth.

Sister Monica understands Hell
to be like this. If overhead cranes clawing
their way through layers of dark air
grew leathery wings and flew screeching
at them, it wouldn't surprise her.
And the three warning whistle blasts,
the blazing orange heat pouring out
liquid fire like Devil's soup
doesn't surprise her—she understands
Industry and Capital and Labor,
the Protestant trinity. That is why
she trembles here, the children clinging
to her as she watches them learn their future.

## Uncle Rudy Explains the Events of 1955

We laid the last course of firebrick
in the big 3-storey kiln when something broke upstairs.
Us brickies on the kiln bottom held our breath
at the first whiff of lime, we knew that stuff
could blind us, burn our lungs.
Each man found another man's hand
before shutting his eyes, so we inched out
that way—like kids, eyes shut tight
and holding hands. Climbed the ladder, finally up
to sweet air, the lime falling like snow
and burning our skin all the way.
That was the winter I found a rabbit
in one of my traps still alive.
The noise he made. "Quit it quit it quit it."
Lord, just like a person. So I quit.

## Uncles' Advice, 1957

My handsome uncles like dark birds
flew away to war. They all flew back
glossier and darker than before, but willing
to be clipped to the mill for reasons
of their own—a pregnant girl,
a business failed, the seductive sound
of accents they'd grown up with—
so they settled, breaking promises to themselves.
This was the time when, moping in my room
while the aunts' voices rose through the floorboards
prophesying my life—stews and babushkas—
the uncles' advice also filtered up
like the smoky, persistent 5-note song
of the mourning dove: get out, don't come back.

## Consumers, 1965

Suddenly they were all rich.
Pickups bloomed with trailer hitches,
outboard motors shone in their driveways.
They'd convoy to the lake, swim and grill steaks
until the men left for 4 to 12's.

Daily, the women had something new to discuss,
but the chrome machines
purring in their kitchens
and the strangeness of old rooms
masked with stiff brocade
unnerved them; frowning, they fingered
drapes and carpets like curators.

They began to pack fat onto bellies and thighs
as if preparing for a long journey on foot
through a frozen country, a journey
they would have to take alone and without provision.

*Lessons*

Aunt Julie's hands knot and whiten
as she squeezes cucumber slices
handful by small handful
into the pale green bowl.

Called away from the uncles
to help in her hot kitchen,
I am beginning to learn
the woman's part. The man's part

is no better. After his mill shift
Uncle Vernon will stand at the back door,
shaky and black. He likes

cucumber salad, so this is the least
Aunt Julie can do: wringing the slices
as if they are somebody's neck.

## The Rope

Their voices still wake me
as I woke for years to that rise and fall,
the rope pulled taut between them,

both afraid to break or let go.
Years spilled on the kitchen table,
picked over like beans or old bills.

What he owed to the mill, what she wanted
for him. Tears swallowed and hidden
under layers of paint, under linoleum rugs,

new piled on old, each year the pattern
brighter, costlier. *The kids*
he would say, *if it weren't for*

She'd hush him and promise
to smile, saying *This is what*
*I want, this is all I ever wanted.*

STEPHEN DUNN

*Hard Work*

1956

At the Coke plant, toting empties
in large crates to the assembly line
I envied my friends away at camp,
but the money was good
and hard work, my father said,
was how you became a man.
I saw a man for no special reason
piss into a coke bottle
and put it back onto the line.
After a while I, too, hated
the bottles enough to break some
deliberately, and smile
and share with the other workers
a petty act of free will.
When I came home at night my body
hurt with that righteous hurt
men have brought home for centuries,
the hurt that demands
food and solicitation, that makes men
separate, lost.
I quit before the summer was over,
exercised the prerogatives of my class
by playing ball all August
and spent the money I'd earned
on Barbara Winokur, who was beautiful.
And now I think my job
must be phased out, a machine must
do it, though someone for sure
still does the hard work of boredom
and that person can't escape,
goes there each morning
and comes home each night
and probably has no opportunity
to say who he is

through destruction, some big
mechanical eye watching him
or some time and motion man
or just something hesitant, some father
or husband, in himself.

## Numbers

The sky turns
an illuminated grey
this afternoon
behind each window of the house

suspended like an amulet

and I am waiting in my kitchen
drinking tea
waiting for the latest
news.

Among other things today
hope was officially forbidden
78 miners
nine hundred feet down.

It is easy to feel
the necessary sorrow

this formal tragedy of ciphers
coming as it does
at 5 o'clock
from a white cube of abstractions

the radio
placed casually
crossways on the refrigerator.

Later commentators
will assure me
it was a day like all days.
I will have had another
cup of pale tea
drifting between what is common
in the black jeweled earth

                    of west virginia
and this grey sky

                    And at other times
I may stop
trying to understand the words
for a number of men
a number of feet deep
                    isolated as this
                    afternoon echo
                    of water falling in a sink

as the radio begins knowingly
                    dealing in numbers.

## The Triangle Fire

### I. Havdallah

This is the great divide
by which God split
the world:
on the Sabbath side
he granted rest,
eternal toiling
on the workday side.

But even one
revolution of the world
is an empty promise
where bosses
where bills to pay
respect no heavenly bargains.
Until each day is ours

let us pour
darkness in a dish
and set it on fire,
bless those who labor
as we pray, praise God
his holy name,
strike for the rest.

### 2. Among the Dead

First a lace of smoke
decorated the air of the workroom,
the far wall unfolded
into fire. The elevator shaft
spun out flames like a bobbin,
the last car sank.

72

I leaped for the cable,
my only chance. Woven steel
burned my hands as I wound
to the bottom.

I opened my eyes. I was lying
in the street. Water and blood
washed the cobbles, the sky
rained ash. A pair of shoes
lay beside me, in them
two blistered feet.
I saw the weave in the fabric
of a girl's good coat,
the wilted nosegay pinned to her collar.
Not flowers, what I breathed then,
awake among the dead.


### 3. Asch Building

In a window,
lovers embrace
haloed by light.
He kisses her, holds her
gently, lets her go
nine stories to the street.

Even the small ones
put on weight
as they fall:
eleven thousand pounds split
the fireman's net,
implode the deadlights

on the Greene Street side,
until the basement catches them

and holds. Here
two faceless ones are found
folded neatly over the steam pipes
like dropped rags.

I like the one
on that smoky ledge, taking stock
in the sky's deliberate mirror.
She gives her hat
to wind, noting its style,
spills her week's pay

from its envelope, a joke
on those who pretend
heaven provides, and chooses
where there is no choice
to marry air, to make
a disposition of her life.


### 4. Personal Effects

One lady's
handbag, containing
rosary beads, elevated
railroad ticket, small pin
with picture, pocket knife,
one small purse containing
$1.68 in cash,
handkerchiefs,
a small mirror, a pair of gloves,
two thimbles, a Spanish
comb, one yellow metal ring,
five keys, one
fancy glove button,

one lady's handbag containing
one gent's watch case
number of movement 6418593
and a $1 bill,
one half dozen postal cards,
a buttonhook, a man's photo,
a man's garter,
a razor strap,
one portion of limb and hair
of human being.


### 5. Industrialist's Dream

This one's
dependable won't
fall apart
under pressure doesn't
lie down on the job
doesn't leave early
come late
won't join unions
strike
ask for a raise
unlike one hundred
forty six
others I could name
who couldn't
take the heat this one's
still at her machine
and doubtless
of spotless moral
character you
can tell by the bones
pure white

this one
does what she's told
and you don't hear
her complaining.


### 6. The Witness

Woman, I might have watched you
sashay down Washington Street
some warm spring evening
when work let out,
your one thin dress
finally right for the weather,
an ankle pretty
as any flower's stem, full
breasts the moon's envy, eyes bold
or modest as you passed me by.

I might have thought, as heat
climbed from the pavement,
what soft work you'd make
for a man like me:
even the time clock, thief of hours,
kinder, and the long day
passing in a dream.
Cradled in that dream
I might have slept
forever, but today's nightmare
vision woke me:
your arms aflame, wings
of fire, and you a falling star,
a terrible lump of coal
in the burning street.
No dream, your hair of smoke,
your blackened face.

No dream the fist I make,
taking your hand
of ashes in my own.


## 7. Cortege

A cold rain comforts the sky.
Everything ash-colored under clouds.
I take my place in the crowd,

move without will as the procession moves,
a gray wave breaking against the street.
Up ahead, one hundred and forty seven

coffins float, wreckage of lives. I follow
the box without a name. In it
whose hand encloses whose heart? Whose mouth

presses the air toward a scream?
She is no one, the one I claim
as sister. When the familiar is tagged

and taken away, she remains.
I do not mourn her. I mourn no one.
I do not praise her. No one

is left to praise. Seventy years after
her death, I walk in March rain behind her.
She travels before me into the dark.


Editors' note: For a historical background of the Triangle Fire, see p. 148.

## In Coal

The sun gets up and lords it
over the stooped hills. Below him
Brood and Blue, those bent old women,
shake out their sooty aprons at the town.

Going out, my husband lifts
his arm against the light
that hurts his eyes.
Last night he saw timbers falling
in his sleep, his hands
digging air as if it was dirt.

I've sunk all I've got in that mine.
All day I feel its mouth at my neck
like some rich old landlord
I owe back rent.
I'll spend this morning sweeping
dust out of the shack.
It's the one thing I can count on
sure to come back.

Tonight when sky turns anthracite
and one star burns, a miner's lamp,
I'll take my wish to the gate
and wait for him
to rise one more time. He'll have
two dollars in his pocket,
a coal-black face. He'll be wearing
the moon in his mouth.

## Picket Line in Autumn

The face getting brown
as morning falls
just ripe out of the sky—
a change from last night's
cold, warm gloves and
frost poured into
these empty coffee cups—

you've never been so much
in the world as now,
spending all daylight
and all night too outdoors,
going in circles like the world does,
though sometimes it seems
standing still, getting nowhere—

except you know your tired feet
are turning the earth
and someday the sun
will give itself up to you,
the leaves surrender—
you know they will, if
you keep on walking long enough.

## Not Working

"a man of your experience" they say
offering nothing
and him laboring forty years

as though to have bread on the table
were enough
he should sit up and beg for that
the bastards

and them so smug, smiling
holding out their soft hands
as if they knew what hands were for

he knows:
not for nothing he's worked
these calluses into his palms, the flesh
hard and ungentle

it's not work he needs
but his own name spoken here
and thoughts that go down
easy and soundless
as the beer in this glass

## Out-of-Luck, Massachusetts

The town that couldn't be licked
gives up, sunk
between these hills. The sacred
heart beats fainter, blessing the poor
in spirit. Boarded-up
factories litter the river. It does no good,
town fathers knitting their brows,
there's not enough shoe leather left
to buy a meal. In company houses
the unemployed wear out
their welcome. Diminished
roads run east, west, anywhere
better than here.

## The Women Who Clean Fish

The women who clean fish are all named Rose
or Grace. They wake up close to the water,
damp and dreamy beneath white sheets,
thinking of white beaches.

It is always humid where they work.
Under plastic aprons, their breasts
foam and bubble. They wear old clothes
because the smell will never go.

On the floor, chlorine.
On the window, dry streams left by gulls.
When tourists come to watch them
working over belts of cod and hake,
they don't look up.

They stand above the gutter. When the belt starts
they pack the bodies in, ten per box,
their tails crisscrossed as if in sacrament.
The dead fish fall compliantly.

It is the iridescent scales that stick,
clinging to cheek and wrist,
lighting up hours later in a dark room.

The packers say they feel orange spawn
between their fingers, the smell of themselves
more like salt than peach.

## Black Money

His lungs heaving all day in a sulphur mist,
then dusk, the lunch pail torn from him
before he reaches the house, his children
a cloud of swallows about him.
At the stove in the tumbled rooms, the wife,
her back the wall he fights most, and she
with no weapon but silence
and to keep him from the bed.

In their sleep the mill hums and turns
at the edge of water. Blue smoke
swells the night and they drift
from the graves they have made for each other,
float out from the open-mouthed sleep
of their children, past banks and businesses,
the used car lots, liquor store, the swings in the park.

The mill burns on, now a burst of cinders,
now whistles screaming down the bay, saws jagged
in half light. Then like a whip
the sun across the bed, windows high with mountains
and the sleepers fallen to pillows
as gulls fall, tilting
against their shadows on the log booms.
Again the trucks shudder the wood framed houses
passing to the mill. My father
snorts, splashes in the bathroom,
throws open our doors to cowboy music
on the radio, hearts are cheating,
somebody is alone, there's blood in Tulsa.
Out the back yard the night-shift men rattle
the gravel in the alley going home.
My father fits goggles to his head.

From his pocket he takes anything metal,
the pearl-handled jack knife, a ring of keys,

and for us, black money shoveled
from the sulphur pyramids heaped in the distance
like yellow gold. Coffee bottle tucked in his armpit
he swaggers past the chicken coop,
a pack of cards at his breast.
In a fan of light beyond him
the Kino Maru pulls out for Seattle,
some black star climbing
the deep globe of his eye.

### 3 A.M. *Kitchen:*
### *My Father Talking*

For years it was land working me, oil fields,
cotton fields, then I got some land. I
worked it. Them days you could just about
make a living. I was logging.

Then I sent to Missouri. Momma
come out. We got married.
We got some kids. Five kids.
That kept us going.

We bought some land near the water.
It was cheap then. The water
was right there. You just looked out
the window. It never left the window.

I bought a boat. Fourteen footer.
There was fish out there then.
You remember, we used to catch
six, eight fish, clean them right
out in the yard. I could of fished to China.

I quit the woods. One day just
walked out, took off my corks, said that's
it. I went to the docks.
I was driving winch. You had to watch
to see nothing fell out of the sling. If
you killed somebody you'd
never forget it. All
those years I was just working
I was on edge, every day. Just working.

You kids, I could tell you
a lot. But I won't.

It's winter. I play a lot of cards
down at the tavern. Your mother.
I have to think of excuses
to get out of the house. You're
wasting your time, she says. You're wasting
your money.

You don't have no idea, Threasie.
I run out of things
to work for. Hell, why shouldn't I
play cards? Threasie,
some days now I just don't know.

## A Photo of Miners

(USA, 1908)

With trees backing them
instead of the pit's mouth,
they could have been
at a fifth-grade picnic.
But the spitballer won't grow into
his father's jacket, and a ladder
of safety pins climbs the front of
the class clown. Stretch,
who got tall the soonest,
has the air of a chimney sweep,
and here is a little grandfather
in brogans and rag gloves,
his face shoved between two shoulders
his arms are draping,
his eyes flashing the riding lights
of pain. They are a year's
supply, average age, give or take
a year: ten. Don't look for
a bare foot at a devil-may-care
angle on one of the rails,
or a habitable face for a life
you might have led—that
mouth is rigid as a mail slot,
the light on those hands predicts
common graves. Does anything transcend
the walleyed patience of beasts,
the artless smirk on the boy
with the high forehead
who thinks he will croon his way
out of this?

## Ice Cream Factory

We keep our cool rhythm
under Jack the foreman's nervous fingers:
Pink the fat man mixes the mix
that Angus pours in molds from six
shiny tits, and I work the stick machine
on this dedicated second shift—
a long way from Veblen and Mann,
and the blonde from Cicero
who, at the last minute last spring,
called her body off the ledge
we'd learned to cling to—
but if I don't think about it I'm OK.
Would my friend Ernest say that?—
say push the button, gain your sticks,
lay them neat for Angus
in the mold, in the brine,
in the line that ends where Millie
takes the frozen bars off the racks,
slips on their paper jackets,
packs them in a box for Stan—
who stacks it in the freezer,
puffed up with summer cold?

I say bulky thought, Ernest.
And bulkier still
when the line shuts down at ten o'clock
and everyone goes home.
Everyone, that is, but Millie and Jack—
they'll meet on the sugar sacks;
and the blonde from Cicero,
her hair screaming,
will continue to fall back through space.

## JOHN GIORNO

## *An Unemployed Machinist*

1964

An unemployed
machinist
An unemployed machinist
who traveled
here
who traveled here
from Georgia
from Georgia 10 days ago
10 days ago
and could not find
a job
and could not find a job
walked
into a police station
walked into a police station
yesterday and said:
yesterday
and said:

"I'm tired
of being scared
I'm tired of being scared."

## He Was When He Died

> The dead man was "an unemployed
> mattress factory worker."
> —*San Francisco Chronicle*
> June 28, 1981

Not president of Inland Steel
or the International Monetary Fund.
Not engaged in price-fixing
or planning the Hudson River Valley
breeder reactor. He was not breeding
racehorses. He did not suffer
from dental caries at the time
of his death. He did not meet death
in the arms of an art historian.
Not under indictment by the IRS
nor under investigation by the SEC.
When he died, it was not the first time
he was absent from the annual encampment
at the Bohemian Grove. Nor was he
stuffing ticking at the mattress factory.

At the time of his death he was not
concerned with a faltering professional
practice, nor did he leave an unfinished
painting of water lilies. Fantastic swirls
of red and blue tatoo did not cover
84% of his body. He died,
not at the mattress factory
where he didn't work. He died
not doing so many things,
it's clear his life was thickly textured,
deep. Uncommonly rich.

Mornings he breakfasted at the Bulky Burger,
one egg on a corn muffin and two links.
Being unemployed at the mattress factory,

he couldn't afford it, but he ate
with no sense of guilt, revealing his complex
understanding of free will. No need
to pity him: he was not a member
of an oppressed minority,
not on a disability pension,
not long out of love, no sort of scapegoat,
not working at the Sleeprite factory
on Cowan Road or the Simmons factory
on Fairway Drive or the Sealy Company
on 7th Street in Richmond or even
at any mattress factory where he
ever had worked. He was, at the time
of his death, not

DONALD HALL

## The Foundations of American Industry

In the Ford plant
at Ypsilanti
men named for their
fathers work at steel
machines named Bliss,
Olaffson, Smith-Grieg,
and Safety.

In the Ford plant
the generators
move quickly on
belts, a thousand now
an hour. New men
move to the belt when
the shift comes.

For the most part
the men are young and
go home to their
Fords, and drive around,
or watch T V,
sleep, and then go to work,
towards payday;

when they walk home
they walk on sidewalks
marked W
P A 38;
their old men made
them, and they walk on
their fathers.

## Machinist

The milling machine
Bleeds curled shavings
Bleeds watery milk onto my shoes

Ceiling fans churn
Air like cream through the room

In my lungs a dray horse
Pauses to shit
Then draws ragged furrows

And in the anthill of my head
Black hands drag
Bone chips and dead flesh from tunnels

Pictures hang on the gray walls
A nailhead spreading
Rust on wet pine
A tarnished key in a drawer
A hubcap cupping its
Small forest of weeds in a ditch

The milled pieces rattle
Into a bin
Shining surfaces unbruised
Waiting to bruise
I never wanted this skill
I wanted a life
And when the end of it comes
I won't be ready
They'll have to bury me

*The One Song*

4. *Polaroid*

He must have thrown it
In his tool box
The evening he brought it home.
I've borrowed it from my mother
To make a copy.
A web of white mars
The black mass that is a shadow
Cast by his milling machine.
A double line of scratches
Runs from his shoulder down his apron
Until it has crossed his heart.
A stain like a cottonball
Covers a secret wound on his temple.

The one who took the picture
Didn't care enough to smear
The whole surface with fixer;
The edges of the scene
Are fading into a world of the lost.
I'll have an impossible time
In the darkroom,
Cursing in the amber cone of light,
Bending to the image
That will blossom in the tray.

But mutilated as the picture is,
It tells a story:
There is a man,
There is a machine,
There is a cart of oily tools,
A hard cold light is falling.

## 9. *The Last Check*

A tool maker.
Surely that must be
The world's oldest profession.

His foreman,
Red-eyed and blowing his nose,
Drops by the house at noon
to leave the instruments of his craft:
Two calipers,
A micrometer,
Gadgets with dial gauges
I can't even guess the use of,
All of them slippery
As live bait
In their fine film of oil.

In another poem, at another time,
I said, father,
He is my father,
Locked in a factory.

Now he has broken out the hard way,
And I have no father.

The mail slot rattles,
And with oiled fingertips
I bring to mother
This day's bundle of sympathy cards.
Among them she finds
His last check.
Thirty-nine years,
For Christ's sweet sake,
And he's been docked vacation pay.

For the one day he took
To die on.

Thirty-nine years, I tell you.
I'm not about to forgive them.
Not now,
Not thirty-nine years from now.

## Printing Press No. 17

my machine
        is a *he;*
everyone else
        has a woman-machine; they say
"there, i've got her
        going now" or "this sure is

a whore of a machine," but *my* machine
    is a man.
i *know* because
    he's so mean to me—
he won't turn out words
but just sits there
        & turns black
& sticky
so i have to
    wash him off:
my machine is a man,
i *know,* even though
he's the first machine
        i've ever met
because he's always
        buggering things up:
i think i'll call him
Adolph or Idi.

## One Day the Sand-Machine

one day the sand-machine
   fell down & almost killed
      Devi & me.

i was going along
  quite happily
breathing in a ton of dust
getting a rash from the glue
getting hunks of metal
              in my eye
being bossed around
               by everyone
& feeling proud
        to have a job
  when bang!
        i met my waterloo (translate sand-loo if you prefer)

i had even
        gotten used to the foreman
(who reminded me of my latest boyfriend
      only with shorter hair—I'm sure
if i had followed
       my boyfriend's orders
we would've gotten along
        quite well too; i also
got used to
      the intricate process
by which people were
           accepted to work at the place
it reminded me of certain communal houses
   and how people could stay
              or not stay
  (only with a good deal
            more fairness)
as i say,
      i was going along quite happily:

a foreman like my boyfriend
a factory like my communal house
a woman to work with
                    who acted like my mother—
        what else could anyone
                    ask for?
when bang! the sand-machine
                        fell down beside me.
    all 2 tons of it.
    Devi jumped back
            white & shaken.
i looked at it
            and ran away
(i thought that it
                was going to blow up)

and everybody actually
                    stopped work
for 15 minutes
            to see if we were dead.

the foreman came in
            and gave me a long lecture
and tried to make it
            sound like my fault;
the East Indian man
                was made to crank up
    the machine again
    (never mind if he got killed)

and afterwards,
                when it was all over
        (& after the foreman's lecture)
Devi winked at me & said
    "He talk too much
    he should do more work."

## The Day After I Quit

the day after
          i quit
i phoned
          Workman's
Compensation
               to get them to send
a health & safety
                    inspector:

   "the glue gives you a rash
   the glass cuts your hands
   the loud crashing noises
      are bad for your hearing
   the heat makes you sick
   pieces of metal
                 get in people's eyes
   someone almost cut off
                    their fingers on the bar-cutter
   the sand-machine
      fell down
   & almost killed me
   & the company won't
      buy a fan"
                 i said


"Well, maybe i'll send an inspector"
   he said, grudgingly, "I'm busy checking out
a construction site." he couldn't believe
      women's jobs were danger
                 -us.

## The Sweatshop Poem

There are thirty-one shallow graves in August
with thirty-one swollen coffins, waiting.

During the day I work in a sweatshop
sewing the pink slips and cotton dresses,
the cashmere skirts and thick tweeds
of winter. During the day my fingers
hum with needles, the needles slide
through patches of steaming cloth.
I am preparing the hottest iron.
I am preparing the warmest clothes
for the beautiful thighs of young models
and the sweating hips of new mannequins.
All day I am prepared for leaving.

And at night the factory is silent.
My tired face dims in the window, my
shadow paces through the empty corridors,
alone. At night the cloth in my hands
never whispers with other men's dreams
or purrs with other women's secrets.
My exhausted body is too heavy for clothes.
All night the heavy tongue of summer repeats
its one heavy syllable, its one drooling
syllable of stupor; the crystal glass
of another night asks me to drink.
And I do drink, deeply.
And later I lie in the naked sheets
without sleeping, without breaking the door
or plunging into the river. Without screaming.

But sometimes I move through the house, slowly.
Sometimes I sit in the dark kitchen

or stand at the swollen bathroom window
to watch the glistening blue worm,
the invisible needle of moonlight
sewing a dark shroud for my body.

## Factories

for Susan Stewart

Everywhere in New York City there are factories
flinging their broken windows into the streets
raining sawdust and glass crying out with the
soft voices of women whispering Puerto Rican names
whispering my name and wearing their dark shadows
like petticoats and their graffiti like too much makeup
over their scarred bricks their used up bodies

they are always stained they have walls
broken off like the stumps of cripples
I'm sorry but this is how it is with me
everywhere I turn I find the ruined mouths
and damp animals of yes and when
I lie down to sleep at night I hear

dry pistons setting into motion like
galloping horses their hooves are echoing
on concrete their iron hearts are hammering
they are churning like diesels bursting out of
tunnels out of mountains out of factories
and shedding silence like an extra skin
pumping blood through the stillness of my arteries

## Driving through
## Coal Country in Pennsylvania,

sometimes you come on a whole
valley that's one gray excavation.
Each valley saddens me.
It's like seeing someone you know
but can hardly recognize anymore,
scarred up, shaved, sick
from a long operation,
only the operation's still going on,
and there are no doctors—
just dump trucks in the distance
raising dust.

## The Milltown Union Bar

Laundromat & Cafe

You could love here, not the lovely goat
in plexiglass nor the elk shot
in the middle of a joke, but honest drunks,
crossed swords above the bar, three men hung
in the bad painting, others riding off
on the phony green horizon. The owner,
fresh from orphan wars, loves too
but bad as you. He keeps improving things
but can't cut the bodies down.

You never need leave. Money or a story
brings you booze. The elk is grinning
and the goat says go so tenderly
you hear him through the glass. If you weep
deer heads weep. Sing and the orphanage
announces plans for your release. A train
goes by and ditches jump. You were nothing
going in and now you kiss your hand.

When mills shut down, when the worst drunk
says finally I'm stone, three men still hang
painted badly from a leafless tree, you
one of them, brains tied behind your back,
swinging for your sin. Or you swing
with goats and elk. Doors of orphanages
finally swing out and here you open in.

## Degrees of Gray in Philipsburg

You might come here Sunday on a whim.
Say your life broke down. The last good kiss
you had was years ago. You walk these streets
laid out by the insane, past hotels
that didn't last, bars that did, the tortured try
of local drivers to accelerate their lives.
Only the churches are kept up. The jail
turned 70 this year. The only prisoner
is always in, not knowing what he's done.

The principal supporting business now
is rage. Hatred of the various grays
the mountain sends, hatred of the mill,
The Silver Bill repeal, the best liked girls
who leave each year for Butte. One good
restaurant and bars can't wipe the boredom out.
The 1907 boom, eight going silver mines,
a dance floor built on springs—
all memory resolves itself in a gaze,
in panoramic green you know the cattle eat
or two stacks high above the town,
two dead kilns, the huge mill in collapse
for fifty years that won't fall finally down.

Isn't this your life? That ancient kiss
still burning out your eyes? Isn't this defeat
so accurate, the church bell simply seems
a pure announcement: ring and no one comes?
Don't empty houses ring? Are magnesium
and scorn sufficient to support a town,
not just Philipsburg, but towns
of towering blondes, good jazz and booze
the world will never let you have
until the town you came from dies inside?

Say no to yourself. The old man, twenty
when the jail was built, still laughs
although his lips collapse. Someday soon,
he says, I'll go to sleep and not wake up.
You tell him no. You're talking to yourself.
The car that brought you here still runs.
The money you buy lunch with,
no matter where it's mined, is silver
and the girl who serves your food
is slender and her red hair lights the wall.

## Get the Gasworks

Get the gasworks into a poem
and you've got the smoke and smokestacks,
the mottled red and yellow tenements,
and grimy kids who curse with the pungency
of the odor of gas. You've got America, boy.

Sketch in the river and barges,
all dirty and slimy.
How do the seagulls stay so white?
And always cawing like little mad geniuses?
You've got the kind of living
that makes the kind of thinking we do:
gaswork smokestack whistle tooting wisecracks.

They don't come because we like it that way,
but because we find it outside our window every morning,
in soot on the furniture,
and trucks carrying coal for gas,
the kid hot after the ball under the wheel.
He gets it over the belly, all right.
He dies there.

So the kids keep tossing the ball around
after the funeral.
So the cops keep chasing them,
so the mamas keep hollering,
and papa flings his newspaper outward,
in disgust with discipline.

## The Gentle Weight Lifter

Every man to his kind of welcome in the world,
some by lifting cement barrels, laboring.
He looks so stupid doing it, we say.
Why not a soft job, pushing a pencil
or racketeering, the numbers game?
As the pattern is rigged, he must
get love and honor lifting barrels.

It would be good to see a change,
but after barrels he cannot fool with intangibles.
He could with his muscular arm sweep them aside
and snarl up the tiny lines by which he can
distinguish love.

He is fixed in his form,
save a hand reach from outside
to pick him up bodily and place him,
still making the movements that insure his love,
amidst wonders not yet arrived.

## The Boss

who hoarded among the monthly bank statements
nude photos,
the drawer locked,
the key in his pocket,
still could complain
of the stupidity of his help—
their incompetency,
their secretiveness;
he could sense it
in their guarded snickers
when he criticized;
who could walk the shop
in possession as he walked,
stoop-shouldered, careless
how he went, sagging;
it was his shop
and his machinery
and his steel cabinet
where the photos lay.

## The Paper Cutter

He slides the cut paper out
from under the raised knife.
His face does not lose interest.
"And now I go to my night job,"
he says cheerfully at five,
wiping his hands upon a rag.
He has stood all day in one spot,
pressing first the left
and then the right button.
"And what are you going to do
with all that money?" I ask.
His shoulders stick out bony.
"I will buy a house
and then I will lie down in it
and not get up all day," he laughs.

# TODD JAILER

## *Paul Haber*

I have worked for the utility 23 years
installing poles and wires, manipulating
high voltage with long fiberglass sticks,
and except for the seven years under
that viper of a foreman Johnson, life
hasn't been too hard. There's been time for
a quick hand of gin, a cold one
at quitting time. Not to say it's been
cake—my back argues with that,
and my fingers when it's damp. Hunting
through turkey and deer season, my Harley
in summer, these were the signs of freedom
and ease I struggled for. In four
weeks it was all shot to hell.
My father died, then my brother-in-law, and
my daughter left high school pregnant to marry
a boy who wants to start a landscaping business.
Landscaping—where's the money in that? Here
I am in this hospital, 47 years and two heart
attacks old, nothing to show but some flowers
from the union and a refrigerator full of deer meat.
The doctor says I'll be working again in six months,
but for what, I don't know.

## Randall Holmes

I was the first Black hired, and until
last year, the only one to make lineman.
Jeez-o-man they gave me shit. My third winter
I got so fed up I showed one racist farmboy, showed
him not to mess with me. He was up a pole,
snow flying, dropping 18 inch bolts and
insulators all over my head. So I cut the guy
wire. That yellow pine went boomeranging back
and forth like a metronome gone crazy, him
clinging to the top for dear life. Jeez-o-man.
Then when the younger Brothers—Teddy & Ben &
Steve—come in talking Black Power, well,
things got easier. They still give me dirty
jobs, but they don't bitch when I stretch them out.
By the book a job can last longer than
an all day safety meeting. They give me that look,
but they don't want no incidents. That
farmboy is a foreman now. And do you know
he hasn't spoken a word to me in
seventeen years? It's only right.

## Bill Hastings

Listen to me, college boy, you can
keep your museums and poetry and string quartets
'cause there's nothing more beautiful than
line work. Clamp your jaws together
and listen:
    It's a windy night, you're freezing the teeth out
of your zipper in the ten below, working stiff
jointed and dreaming of Acapulco, the truck cab.
Can't keep your footing for the ice, and
even the geese who died to fill your vest
are sorry you answered the call-out tonight.
You drop a connector and curses
take to the air like sparrows who freeze
and fall back dead at your feet.
Finally you slam the SMD fuse home.
Bang! The whole valley lights up below you
where before was unbreathing darkness.
In one of those houses a little girl
stops shivering. Now that's beautiful,
and it's all because of you.

## Chester Gleason

Here I am up in the cherry picker enjoying the view
when this crazed squirrel comes charging at me like
a chicken with the screaming meemees, jumps claws
out over the crank so I duck down in the bucket
except my sleeves tangle around the upper boom control
and me and the squirrel go gazooming up into the main
trunk and leaves are raining, branches crackling and
the hand line gets taut with the come-along caught
on the service bank, kaboom, and I can't go for
the controls with a rabid squirrel scrabbling
around my hard hat, pissing down my collar, 'til
finally that nutola takes a leap for the greenery
but now the bucket won't work and I got to shimmy
down the boom all stinking with squirrel piss
and the guys rolling around on the hystericals
when this lady comes stomping out all bleary and lion
eyed about her Methuselah tree, and hell no I won't
fill out an accident report I'm going home.

## Time and a Half

Overtime is a delicacy gobbled
by family men who wipe their mouths
and say Baby needs new shoes.
Whether it's a three hour truck trip
to the mechanics and back, or an hour
plowing the parking lot, Baby
needs new shoes. Some drunk demolishes
a pole and we rise to a 3 A.M.
call-out muttering new shoes baby
new shoes. After 23 hours repairing
ice storm damage, the lineman
falls into bed and dreams
of watching his children grow
out of their shoes.

## The Aesthetics of Line Work

We spend all afternoon hanging
the 3-phase bank of transformers.
Notice the flat futuristic curve
of the common neutral, the perfectly
straight 1/ought copper risers
in parallel, the unobtrusive
bulge of the taped connectors.
The lineman squints, hands on
hips, "I'm gonna bring the wife
and kids around to see this
on Sunday," he says, only half
joking.

EXCERPT FROM
*From America:*
*A Poem in Process*


Lexington, Kentucky

I wish I was a horse
had me a groom
a stable boy a jockey
and a master starve himself
to buy me hay
I wish I was a horse
had me plantations full of grass
for grazing and a swimming pool
and one helluva pretty city
upside down to watch me race
some other horse
every now and then

I wish I was a horse
couldn't read about nothing
couldn't read about some local boy
the daily papers
said they asked him what kind of school he'd
like
the boy said he'd "rather just
be hit by a truck" what
kind of a fool boy is that
in Lexington Kentucky
there's a railroad crossing
holds down traffic to a lengthy idle
while
the coal cars trundle through
The Burlington Northern
coal cars weighing 200,000 pounds each
coal cars carrying its weight again 200,000 pounds
of coal: I reckon takes good track to carry that
a heavy rail

I hear they throw on up to three of them high-
powered engines each one 450,000 pounds at 3/4 of a million
dollars each to pull 100 coal cars taking the goodies
out of Eastern Kentucky
where the only respite for the two-legged
variety of inhabitant is serious or fatal
injury
where
in relationship to The Red River North and The Red
Lake River flowing North
am I
too small
to change anything at all?

## I Had No More to Say

The last time I saw her
this flat
above the 7-Up Cadillac Bar—
empty now, windows closed
and covered with dust—
was a coffee house
to which I came
because I knew she'd
be there.
At the window, away
from the others,
she told me about
her mother, always
alone, her father
somewhere else,
in a hotel, in a bar,
her sister who hated
everything.
I told her about
Dodge Truck.
How I swung differentials,
greased bearings,
lifted hubs to axle casings
in 110° heat.
How the repairman said nothing
as he watched me
almost lose two fingers.
Although she did
not answer, her face
tensed and her eyes
told me, Don't
be afraid, it
won't last forever.
I had no more to say.
I took her hand,
walked to the center

of the room. As voices
on the phonograph sang
we turned, descended
in one beat, rose,
shifted and shifted again.
I sang to her
like the song.
I forgot
what the morning
would bring; the early
bus ride, nervousness,
the factory.

## Between Us

What was his name?
Drank gin from
a used paper cup, wasn't
even break time yet.
Sitting on a Hi-Lo, his
muscled arms hung
over the wheel.

        Between us
white dust covered
with sulphur, the dream
of a farm.
"In a few years ought to have
five head of cattle
and a tractor."

9 years and 283 miles
to the south side, the voices
in the Whole Truth Mission
singing gospel. "But I
came right here to
Mt. Elliot Street.
Wasn't no future
praisin' Jesus."

## Fog

All day the air was fog;
couldn't see
the barbed wire, rusting
scraps, stacks
and stacks of pallets,
the tarpaper roof
of Dreamer's shack,
the underground
caverns of salt hardening
around bones.

      The fog says,
Who will save
Detroit now?
A toothless face
in a window shakes No,
sore fingers
that want to be still
say, Not me.
Not far away from where
Youmna lies
freezing in bed,
rolling her eyes, declaring,
This is a place!
the remains of mountains
wait to be moved
through smokestacks
into air.

## Nothing and No One and
## Nowhere to Go

I've laughed before no one,
cried before fire floating
in iron molds, felt
the crow and the peppergrass
against brown dawn.
I never pray "Father" or "Son,"
I scavenge if I have to.
At Hudson Motorcar
an Iraqi I worked with
never talked, except
after the shift began,
he'd kneel and sing
"Allah la ilah." He wanted
mercy, from somewhere
in Arabia, but I never
wanted anything
from the metal rushing
into sand troughs
or the grease
I smelled and breathed.
I've always waited:
for warm rain to wash the sky,
for the woman
beside the river of sludge
to disappear.
Now I wait for the hours left,
alone, shivering,
wait until I can't
hear myself talking to myself
or hear my heart beat
for nothing and no one
and nowhere to go.

## In the Tenth Year of War

I bend
over the machine. Heat
and oil
tune my inner ear. I'm
not ashamed, I
hang my head in
anticipation. Father,
steel smooth and silver,
make my brain new,
Jesus, the dirt on the walls
is coming from my body,
and love,
the spirit coming from your body—
everywhere you look now,
everything you touch,
it's good.
When,
in the tenth year of war
I prayed for help
and no one came,
I danced before the machine.

## Is It You?

Where the giant magnet lifts
pig iron and bales of steel
and a larva dangles
from a spider's thread
beside an old press machine,
where the '53 DeSoto is
among piles of chassis
and transmissions,
and air is wakened
by an ore boat's horn,

someone calls.
Is it you, who numbers stars
the same as Job's
and hides words in my bones
demanding, Count them?
Is it you, calling me,
your blackest rib?

## Father Answers His Adversaries

It's early March, Eisenhower still
president, & Mother's heating up supper
for the third time tonight.
We're at the table doing homework,
& she tells us Father's next in line
for foreman, that today he'll know for sure.
He's three hours late.

Half past eight the Chevy
screeches into the carport.
For a minute, nothing.
Then the sudden slam, & the thump downstairs
to the basement. Beneath our feet
Father lays into the workbench
with a sledgehammer—the jam jars
of nails, of screws, of nuts & bolts
he'd taken years to sort out
exploding against the wall.

Later, sheepish, he comes up,
slumps in his seat & asks for supper.
And when Mother brings his plate
& he looks up at her
& she takes his head on her breast,
he blushes, turns away, & spits out
that final, weary-mouthed answer
to all of it—General Motors & the bosses
& the union pimps & the punched-out Johnnies,
every yes-man goddam ass-lick
who'd ever been jumped to foreman
over him—*aah, crap's like cream,*
*it rises.*

## K Mart

Mother is off to LADIES WEAR,
Father to HOME FURNISHINGS.
As usual, I'm with him.

Passing HARDWARE, he instructs me
in the merits of variable-speed
drills, the sham of saber saws,
the parable of human folly
embodied in third-rate drop-forged
hammers. I nod. I'm twelve. He's
teaching me to shop like a man.

AUTOMOTIVE; SPORTING GOODS
a foray into COSMETICS
for deodorant & shave cream—
the lights droning overhead
their rheumy, incessant gossip,
here, in the one place we talk.

When it's time to go, his lessons
lapse. He wanders off by himself,
whistling his special call for Mother:
two notes
so high & clear they rise
above the whole store—
that tired, adult head, the jowls
rich with ridicule, with affection, Father
floating there like some exotic bird—
calling again & again for his unseen lover
across the abyss of goods between them.

# There Are 23 Steel Mills
## in Buffalo, N.Y.

1.   On summer nights
the stars won't rain,
the red dust will not rise, will not
become a man again:
we can hear it
on the other side of the bedroom wall,
gnawing the clapboard
while we sleep.

Chewed down to its knees,
South Buffalo collapses,
& we ooze through the siding
into the dark, metallic air.

How we've longed for this!—
to lift with the smoke
coiling above the roofs,
to caress one another, at last,
without shame.
                    But we are
ashamed, even in dreams.
Each of us drifts off alone.

2.      Before dawn
we float back to our beds.
The houses clumsily reassemble.
The back yards unclench
& let the moonlight seep through.
The steel mills sing our names
softly; they know who we are.

By 6 we're up
& at breakfast, reading the paper—
whispering as we read,
in wry, submissive voices:

the voice to be used at work
to apologize, to confess,
to exact penance
from every word we know . . .

*Yes.*
*I will.*
*Whatever you say.*
—the words coming on
in piston-strokes
as we slog to the corner
to catch the bus for work,
the words our mouths fill to
over & over, without love
for ourselves or this place
we have made with our own hands.

# Cuba

In my dream, Joey, both of us were alive
& walking in Delaware Park.
The dew glistened on our shoes.
Neither of us spoke of your death.
We talked of other mornings, in winter,
when we'd drive up Hopkins
home from Bethlehem Steel—
two washed-out Marxists, sure suckers
for the good intentions & the dialectic
under every rock. The blue snow
swirled the blue streets of South Buffalo,
& the streetlights hazed into swell-bellied
moons. And to pass the time
you always had a story . . .
about the Navy, or a woman,
or the way the sea shimmered
at night off the Moroccan coast.
Next year, you'd say. Next year for sure
you were going to Cuba, leave the snow
& the mills, cut cane for a living.
Come off it, Joey, I'd say, you'll be lucky
to make it out of the country. And anyway,
I've heard it before—you change your life
more often than your underwear.

Something was always trying to get out
when you'd talk. Friday nights
at Locklin's, you'd be pouring existentialism
down some 15-year-old's throat, your hands
flapping as you talked, your cigarette
weaving a smoky trail of enthusiasm
you could never bring yourself
to believe . . .

    Who needs it.
*Who needs it,* you said

that time after Michael's funeral.
Our backs to the bar, the gang of us
nodded in unison. For once
we believed you, knew what you meant,
all of us stuck with what we knew
we were—sentimental & drunk
& fattening into our thirties.

All winter, brain reamed by booze,
you wanted to die. None of us knew,
though anyone could see it:
that grand gesture of denial
hovering like a ghost just beyond
your skin . . . that it was as close
as you'd ever get to Havana.
Sundays on the West Side, weighing 260,
browsing for a coronary, how you'd hit
the bakeries for cannoli. Or mornings
after work, dreaming you were out in the cane
as we roared up Hopkins in your Olds 88
& you'd lean out the window shouting
*eat dust you bourgeois creeps,*
how it was one jazzy epiphany after another,
Joey, right up to the moment
you shoved the gun in your mouth
& took off.

## Contract Miners

for Big Ed

Underground we fought the earth together.
From the hell of it, and peacock copper.
From the womb she was no tender lover.
The stone-boat rocker wouldn't budge
a crumb to a beggar's cup,
or toss a meatless bone
to a blind man's bitch. Until we made her.
Compressor moan and drill chatter
in her lamp-lit face
forced surrender from the stone.

Midwife to the mine he taught me how
to spit a round and slant a lifter.
He grinned greenhorn at my back
when I smelled fear curl thru the drift
and cling to shaky fingers
as each to each they lit spliced fuses
one by one. And then we ran
down the cross-cut tunnel.
Soon the shudder of ground
brought us back to witness birth.

The mice sat in the corner of our eyes.
We heard them listen
to the timber groan beneath
gravid loins of working earth.
With care and art, mindful of the mice,
we imitated moles. We spiled thru mealy
low grade zones to court her frigid heart,
where once solutions boiled
and, dying darkly, cooled.

## Kelley Shaft Ceremony

In New York City
priests say mass for Cornelius Kelley,
cartel king of copper.
Ground wind in his copper camp howls
winter requiem in Butte.
Half-mast hoist-house flags whip attention
while shifters cream lukewarm lies
into bitter coffee cups.
Cold white skin men dress in drys,
prepare to descend in silent steam.
Shaft lights flicker, helmets click
as someone shuffles on the grate,
a lame Finn drops his bucket,
crowds a Mick.
Both men mutter in the cage
as a company suck
went to ritual at the portal stage.
To honor Kelley
he makes an inscribed copper plate
and screw holes above the shive wheel
in the gallus frame.
Now men slip down the throat
of a dead man's monument.

# Contributor's Note

I rode a motor
thru a tramway tunnel
in the Mountain Con,
listened to the brass
bell clang as the skip
hoist banged the bucket
up the number two shaft.

The Kelly men worked
in the open stope,
barred down rock
from a bald headed raise
to the gopher crews
who mucked around
the goddamn clock.

They coughed up soot
but silica stuck
as the widow-makers howled
when the Ingersoll moaned
and the starter steel struck
the hornblende stone.

I burned images black
on the hanging wall
with a spitter's lamp,
drank brackish water
from a tin-can cup
and grew hands hard
with knotted knuckles.

And I cleaned track
with a moron's claw,

scraped the turnsheet down
with a flat Finn hoe—
bird in an alligator's jaw.

Lost in a drift of teeth
I dreamed a lot.

## *Working: The Egg Keeper*

Riding the fork lift
down long waxed corridors
in shatterproof glasses
iron toed safety shoes
moving blue plastic
past the blinking console
monitoring moon rockets
blue and green raised maps
where continents wrinkle and furrow
the heart and lung machine
a constant electric whine
inside the refrigerator
lights on
blue, infra-red, neon
shining on the eggs
you stack
thin white blue-veined
neat and cold in rows—
the heavy enamel doors close—
zipping up your back packer's jacket
thin as parachute silk, cerise
pink as a flare in the snow.

## *The Everlasting Sunday*

Waiting for it
in line to punch out
or punch in.
Bowed my head
into the cold grey
soup of the wash trough,
talked with men
who couldn't talk, marked
my bread with the black
print of my thumb
and ate it.

Nine-foot lengths
of alloy tubing between
my gloved hands
sliding, and the plop
of the cutter, and again
the tube drawing. Above
like swords, bundles
of steel sliding
in the blackened vaults,
and I, a lone child,
counting out.

Now to awaken,
pace the wood floor.
Through the torn shade
the moon between
the poplars riding
toward morning. My
dark suit, my stiffened
shirt stained
with God knows what,
my tie, my silvered
underwear guarding
the sad bed.

Naked, my hard arms
are thin as a girl's,
my body's hairs tipped
with frost. This house,
this ark of sleeping men,
bobs in the silence. I feel
my fingers curl
but not in anger,
the floor warms,
my eyes fill with light.
When was I young?

## Fist

Iron growing in the dark,
it dreams all night long
and will not work. A flower
that hates God, a child
tearing at itself, this one
closes on nothing.

Friday, late,
Detroit Transmission. If I live
forever, the first clouded light
of dawn will flood me
in the cold streams
north of Pontiac.

It opens and is no longer.
Bud of anger, kinked
tendril of my life, here
in the forged morning
fill with anything—water,
light, blood—but fill.

## Coming Home, Detroit, 1968

A winter Tuesday, the city pouring fire,
Ford Rouge sulfurs the sun, Cadillac, Lincoln,
Chevy gray. The fat stacks
of breweries hold their tongues. Rags,
papers, hands, the stems of birches
dirtied with words.
                              Near the freeway
you stop and wonder what came off,
recall the snowstorm where you lost it all,
the wolverine, the northern bear, the wolf
caught out, ice and steel raining
from the foundries in a shower
of human breath. On sleds in the false sun
the new material rests. One brown child
stares and stares into your frozen eyes
until the lights change and you go
forward to work. The charred faces, the eyes
boarded up, the rubble of innards, the cry
of wet smoke hanging in your throat,
the twisted river stopped at the color of iron.
We burn this city every day.

## Detroit Grease Shop Poem

Four bright steel crosses,
universal joints, plucked
out of the burlap sack—
"the heart of the drive train"—
the book says. Stars
on Lemon's wooden palm,
stars that must be capped,
rolled, and annointed,
that have their orders
and their commands as he
has his.
        Under the blue
hesitant light another day
at Automotive
in the city of dreams.
We're all there to count
and be counted, Lemon,
Rosie, Eugene, Luis,
and me, too young to know
this is for keeps, pinning
on my apron, rolling up
my sleeves.
        The roof leaks
from yesterday's rain,
the waters gather above us
waiting for one mistake.
When a drop falls on Lemon's
corded arm, he looks at it
as though it were something
rare or mysterious
like a drop of water or
a single lucid meteor
fallen slowly from
nowhere and burning on
his skin like a tear.

# They Feed They Lion

Out of burlap sacks, out of bearing butter,
Out of black bean and wet slate bread,
Out of the acids of rage, the candor of tar,
Out of creosote, gasoline, drive shafts, wooden dollies,
They Lion grow.
        Out of the gray hills
Of industrial barns, out of rain, out of bus ride,
West Virginia to Kiss My Ass, out of buried aunties,
Mothers hardening like pounded stumps, out of stumps,
Out of the bones' need to sharpen and the muscles' to stretch,
They Lion grow.
        Earth is eating trees, fence posts,
Gutted cars, earth is calling in her little ones,
"Come home, Come home!" From pig balls,
From the ferocity of pig driven to holiness,
From the furred ear and the full jowl come
The repose of the hung belly, from the purpose
They Lion grow.
        From the sweet glues of the trotters
Come the sweet kinks of the fist, from the full flower
Of the hams the thorax of caves,
From "Bow Down" come "Rise Up,"
Come they Lion from the reeds of shovels,
The grained arm that pulls the hands,
They Lion grow.
        From my five arms and all my hands,
From all my white sins forgiven, they feed,
From my car passing under the stars,
They Lion, from my children inherit,
From the oak turned to a wall, they Lion,
From they sack and they belly opened
And all that was hidden burning on the oil-stained earth
They feed they Lion and he comes.

## You Can Have It

My brother comes home from work
and climbs the stairs to our room.
I can hear the bed groan and his shoes drop
one by one. You can have it, he says.

The moonlight streams in the window
and his unshaven face is whitened
like the face of the moon. He will sleep
long after noon and waken to find me gone.

Thirty years will pass before I remember
that moment when suddenly I knew each man
has one brother who dies when he sleeps
and sleeps when he rises to face this life,

and that together they are only one man
sharing a heart that always labors, hands
yellowed and cracked, a mouth that gasps
for breath and asks, Am I gonna make it?

All night at the ice plant he had fed
the chute its silvery blocks, and then I
stacked cases of orange soda for the children
of Kentucky, one gray box-car at a time

with always two more waiting. We were twenty
for such a short time and always in
the wrong clothes, crusted with dirt
and sweat. I think now we were never twenty.

In 1948 in the city of Detroit, founded
by de la Mothe Cadillac for the distant purpose
of Henry Ford, no one wakened or died,
no one walked the streets or stoked a furnace,

for there was no such year, and now
that year has fallen off all the old newspapers,
calendars, doctors' appointments, bonds,
wedding certificates, driver's licenses.

The city slept. The snow turned to ice.
The ice to standing pools or rivers
racing in the gutters. Then bright grass rose
between the thousands of cracked squares,

and that grass died. I give you back 1948.
I give you all the years from then
to the coming one. Give me back the moon
with its frail light falling across a face.

Give me back my young brother, hard
and furious, with wide shoulders and a curse
for God and burning eyes that look upon
all creation and say, You can have it.

## Sweet Will

The man who stood beside me
34 years ago this night fell
on to the concrete, oily floor
of Detroit Transmission, and we
stepped carefully over him until
he wakened and went back to his press.

It was Friday night, and the others
told me that every Friday he drank
more than he could hold and fell
and he wasn't any dumber for it
so just let him get up at his
own sweet will or he'll hit you.

"At his own sweet will," was just
what the old black man said to me,
and he smiled the smile of one
who is still surprised that dawn
graying the cracked and broken windows
could start us all to singing in the cold.

Stash rose and wiped the back of his head
with a crumpled handkerchief and looked
at his own blood as though it were
dirt and puzzled as to how
it got there and then wiped the ends
of his fingers carefully one at a time

the way the mother wipes the fingers
of a sleeping child, and climbed back
on his wooden soda-pop case to
his punch press and hollered at all
of us over the oceanic roar of work,
addressing us by our names and nations—

"Nigger, Kike, Hunky, River Rat,"
but he gave it a tune, an old tune,
like "America the Beautiful." And he danced
a little two-step and smiled showing
the four stained teeth left in the front
and took another suck of cherry brandy.

In truth it was no longer Friday,
for night had turned to day as it
often does for those who are patient,
so it was Saturday in the year of '48
in the very heart of the city of man
where your Cadillac cars get manufactured.

In truth all those people are dead,
they have gone up to heaven singing
"Time on My Hands" or "Begin the Beguine,"
and the Cadillacs have all gone back
to earth, and nothing that we made
that night is worth more than me.

And in truth I'm not worth a thing
what with my feet and my two bad eyes
and my one long nose and my breath
of old lies and my sad tales of men
who let the earth break them back,
each one, to dirty blood or bloody dirt.

Not worth a thing! Just like it was said
at my magic birth when the stars
collided and fire fell from great space
into great space, and people rose one
by one from cold beds to tend a world
that runs on and on at its own sweet will.

## March 25, 1911

It was Spring. It was Saturday.
Payday. For some it was Sabbath.
Soon it will be Easter. It was
approaching April, nearing Passover.
It was close to closing time.

The heads of trees budding
in Washington Square Park.
The sun a hot flywheel spinning
the earth's axle. The days long
enough for leaving in light.
                    It was Spring.

America's sweethearts—the ladies—
stroll in shirtwaists of lawn and lace,
mimic Charles Dana Gibson's Girls.
They pose in finery cut from bolts of
flimsy and stitched by garment girls
on Gibbs, Wilcox, and Singer machines.
                    It was Saturday.

Up in the Asch Building
in the Triangle Shirtwaist Company
Rosie Glantz is singing "Every Little
Movement Has a Meaning of Its Own."

Author's Note: The Triangle Shirtwaist Company manufactured blouses for women and was located on the eighth, ninth, and tenth floors of the Asch Building, at the corner of Washington Place and Greene Street, in New York City's Washington Square. The company employed up to 900 workers at a time, but on March 25, 1911, only about 500 were present. These were immigrants, most of whom could not speak the English language. Nearly all were female, primarily Russian or Italian, although twelve nationalities were known to be "on the books."

At about 4:45 P.M., just after pay envelopes had been distributed, a fire broke out. Not everyone was able to reach the elevators and stairways. On the ninth floor, because the bosses had kept the doors locked to keep out union organizers, workers were forced to jump from windows. One hundred forty-six people, some as young as fourteen, perished.

Fixing hair, arranging puffs and tendrils,
the other girls in the cloakroom join in:
"Let me call you Sweetheart,
I'm in love with you."
                    It was Payday.

Attar-of-roses, lily of the valley,
still they smell of machine oil
that soaks the motors and floors.
The barrel in each stairwell
could fill a thousand lamps.
                    For some it was Sabbath.

Here at Triangle, Sophie Salemi
and Della Costello sew on Singers.
Neighbors from Cherry Street,
they piecework facing each other,
the oil pan hitting their knees.
Tomorrow sisters will nail flowers
on tenement doors.
                    Soon it will be Easter.

The machine heads connected by belts
to the flywheel to rotating axle
sing the Tarantella. Faster,
faster vibrate the needles, humming
faster the fashionable dance.
                    It was approaching April.

Della and Sophie up on Ninth
piece sleeves, race the needle's pace
not knowing on Eighth, paper patterns
burn from the wire, fall on machines,
spark moths and pinwheels round the room.
Rockets push up cutting-tables.
                    It was nearing Passover.

On Eighth, cutters throw pails of water
on the lawn of flame, and Louis,
holding the canvas hose, hollers:
"No pressure! Nothing coming!"
                    It was close to closing time.

Down on Greene Street, Old Dominick
pushes his wheelbarrow, describes
"a big puff" when windows popped,
glittering showers of glass.
                    It was Spring.

Flaming swords, Pluto piles to Ninth.
Sophie and Della and dozens of others
jump on machine tables; the aisles jammed
with wicker workbaskets and chairs.
                    It was Saturday.

Mrs. Yaller testified: "Some froze at
machines. Others were packed in the cloakroom
filled with smoke. I heard them yelling
in Yiddish or Italian, crying out
the names of their children."
                    It was Payday.

Reporter Bill Shepherd is writing:
"I remember the great strike of last year,
these same girls demanding decent
working conditions."
                    For some it was Sabbath.

Rosie runs to the stairway. The door,
Locked! The telephone. Dead! Piling red
ribbons, fire backs girls into windows.
They stand on sills, see the room
a smashed altar lamp, hear the

screaming novenas of flame.
                    Soon it will be Easter.

Pleats of purple and gold wave,
incandescent filaments of lace snow
in shrapnel of needles and screws.
The blaze from molten bolts stains
glass, walls and lawns—on Cherry Street
sisters nail flowers on tenement doors.
                    It was approaching April.

"I could see them falling,"
said Lena Goldman. "I was sweeping out
front of my cafe. At first we thought
it was bolts of cloth—till they opened
with legs! I still see the day
it rained children. Yes.
                    It was nearly Passover."

Sophie and Della stand on windowsill,
look out the crazy quilt of town:
*We will leave for our*
*block on Cherry Street,*
*leave these skeletons*
*leaning on machines,*
*the faces fixed on black*
*crucifix of cloakroom window.*
                    It was close to closing time.

The *Times* quotes Mr. Porter: "The Triangle
never had a fire drill—only three factories
in the city have. One man I pleaded
with replied, 'Let em burn. They're
a lot of cattle anyhow.' "
                    It was Spring.

151

Sophie and Della stand on sill:
*We will leave, our arms*
*around each other, our only*
*sweethearts. Piling red roses*
*two white hearses pull up*
*Cherry Street and the Children*
*of Mary Society march*
*in banners of prayers.*
It was Saturday.

Captain Henry was the first policeman to arrive:
"I saw dozens of girls hanging from sills.
Others, dresses on fire, leapt from the ledges."
It was Payday.

Sophie and Della look on crazy quilt of town:
*Fifty of our schoolmates*
*sing in procession:*
*O Trinity of Blessed Light*
*Our Lady of Perpetual Help*
*Ave Maria, Ave Maria*
*Now and at the Hour*
*of the Tarantella.*
For some it was Sabbath.

Ordering the nets and ladders, Battalion
Chief Worth explains, "I didn't know
they would come down three and even four
together. Why, these little ones went
through life-nets, pavement and all."
Soon it will be Easter.

Sophie and Della stand on windowsill:
*Look, the flywheel sun sinks*
*in the west. In the Winter*
*Garden, Mr. Jolson springs*

152

*and bows in blackface.*
              It was approaching April.

*At the Metropolitan Opera*
*George M. Cohan struts "The Rose*
*of Tralee" to the rich trailing*
*in diamond-sackcloth, rending*
*green ashes of dollar bills.*
              It was nearing Passover.

Sophie and Della stand on sill,
look down crazy quilt of town:
*Intertwined comets we will stream*
*the nightmares of Triangle Bosses*
*Joseph Asch*
*Max Blanck*
*Isaac Harris.*
              It was close to closing time.

*Our Bosses of the Locked*
*Doors of Sweetheart Contracts*
*who in puffs and tendrils*
*of silent telephones,*
*disconnected hoses, barred*
*shutters, fire escapes*
*dangling in perpetual no*
*help on earth in heaven.*
              It was Spring.

*The Lord is my shepherd*
*green pastures still*
*waters anointest heads*
*with oil overflowing*
*preparest a table—now*
*our arms around each other*
*we thread the needle where*

*no rich man can go spinning*
*the earth's axle we are*
*leaving in light.*

## Triangle Site

Asch Building, 1911; Brown Building, 1981

Soaked to skin, look through lens
at Eighth, Ninth, Tenth. So this
is where they worked, I thought

How hot the loft on summer days
and say aloud the layers learned
from photogravure fashion plates:

Pantaloons, petticoats, hour-glass
corsets, one cover called a camisole.
So many strings! In the spinning

Mills down South, steam looms boomed
and even in Winter children stripped
to their shifts, baby hands slick

On cotton bobbins. The shutter clicks,
a pigeon struts and springs. So this
is where they fell. Or jumped.

Layers billow, catch broken rails,
like sails slap on light posts or
pile high on iron fence spears

Where like a little boat, one
pierced shoe holds a paper rose
stem up.

## Sear

July 1982

Always adding. Revising this manuscript.
I plant *direct quotations* on the page,
arranging line-breaks, versification.

Newspaper files: Frances Perkins speaks
from the street, *I felt I must sear it
not only on my mind but on my heart
forever.* One mother, *When will it be
safe to earn our bread?* Their words.
Yet some call that schmaltz, soap-opera

*Sentiment, Victorian melodrama.* Riding
the subway, smoke fizzes in my ears and
in my room, electric heater coils glow
Cs and Os in the box. To write about *them*
yet not interfere, although I'm told
a poet's task is to create a little world.

A testimony: Two tried to stay together
on the ledge, but one suddenly twisted
and plunged, a burning bundle. The other
looked ahead, arms straight out, speaking
and shouting *as if addressing an invisible
audience.* She gestured an embrace then

Jumped. Her name was Celia
Weintraub. She lived
on Henry Street.

## *Heavy Machinery*

What is poetry for? To tell the man
who has just driven home
too fast from his job at the factory
that what he wants is out of this world,
that the descending sun and materializing moon
weren't installed in his windshield but beyond it,
that his eyes can't fly, that their fluttering lids
are certainly wings but atrophied,
and a steering wheel is the only orbit
he'll ever own? Oh yes. But it should also
give him something consoling to say to the guys
tomorrow at break: no matter how delicate the stars may look
the cosmos is heavy machinery, and much harder to operate
than the kind they work and curse.
And it should tell him the rest: the future
features bedtime, and to go to sleep is to remove
and unfold and let go
of the mind, the levitating blanket.

## Foundryblack

The river of Charon, to the Romans, was Styx,
To the Greeks, blackest Lethe, and to the men and boys
Of Lufkin, Texas, tar-patched Archer Avenue
That separates the foundry complex

From the far shore's rented housefronts:
Condemned neighborhoods that foundrymen go home to.
Archer's crosswalks ferry them there and back.
The Occupational Safety and Health Administration

Inspector's clipboard checklist has no numbers to account for
The noise, the heat, the ungovernable smell:
The dusts, degrees and decibels of Hell.
What gauge of safety lens, what thickness

Of ear protection, or density of regulation gauze mask
Can persuade men to hear, see and speak no evil?
How many hardhats? Units of steel-toed footwear?
Or private "Johnny on the Spot" chemical closets?

A machinist, grade four, leans against a half-smoked
Cigarette, circled in signpaint and halved
By a red warningslash. The G-4 ignites the match
No rule can extinguish: the one lit twenty years ago.

"You weren't *yea* high in them days,"
He tells the man who works beside him,
And makes equal to a boy's height
The distance from his hand to the filthy factory floor.

The pinkest rouge's, or fluffiest talc's perfume,
When he remembers it, or tries, is indistinct.
But other smells, everyday ones, impress and won't dilute:
Smell of the just-struck match; of a flooded engine as it waits.

Of the alleys of burgerkitchens;
Of the air surrounding a choked dumpster
That flies make quick paths in
Like tips of fiddlers' bows. Vanilla,

Sweet behind a girl's ear; nicotine in a woman's hair.
But no smell will have, for him, the permanence
Of foundryblack's: of oily, sulfurred, half-
Incinerated grit ground between machine teeth.

Of what he remembers, too much is black:
Blackest, the hearses that ferried friends away;
Black also, the machine-mashed fingernails—
Dead beforehand—that blackened and replaced themselves

With stronger, flesh-colored deadnesses.
But there's light, too, he won't forget: the boy
Whose clean hand he took and showed the way across.
Walk  Don't Walk  not, on Archer's shores, a lightly taken choice.

SUZANNE MATSON

## Love in the Coal Mine

Once pulled past the black mouth
the girls melted into the sides of their lovers
who knew the slope, the trapdoors, the danger of euphoria.
Unbuttoning the descent with a flashlight
wasn't like choosing a hollow on the beach
where open sandstone cliffs could be your temporary fort
and white light poured through gaps in the blankets.

Love in the coal mine, though damp and hot,
wasn't like wrapping your legs around your love in Lost Lake—
him standing your sliding ground,
you leaning back to float your hair on the water
like a slip of woodsmoke. And underground
you could never find anything like a pair of quick tongues
cricketing by a campfire.

Down there it was a deathless weight
rolled over your eyes, a thickness
that filled your throat, making your breath grow ragged
like an untimbered ceiling. In the airless rooms
you could believe in a flickering, floating way out—
like stiffening vertebrae arching and rising
in the underbellied dark.

## *One Summer*

My father coming home
from the factory
summer and still light out
the green bus at the end
of the endless street
the foul sigh
on which my father stepped down
walking slowly in the shadows
holding my hand
my father tired and frowning
eating his supper of potatoes
reading the Bulletin
news of the war
and columns of boxscores
my father singing lewd hymns
in his tuneless voice
stretched out full length in the tub
his calves hanging over the rim
his long penis resting
on the surface of the grey water

## Seeing Them on Television

The miners' wives and children
come down like shepherds
from the hills,
group themselves as if in a painting

It is not that they are hungry
or clothed in rags,
but their faces are like those
of the imagined poor,
blackened by disaster
and weary from waiting
for news of a miracle

We see them flattened,
a single image,
the ancient crowd of mourners
in a continual passion play,
a tableau behind a voice
that has dropped low enough
for decorum

## Women Whose Lives Are Food, Men Whose Lives Are Money

Mid-morning Monday she is staring
peaceful as the rain in that shallow back yard
she wears flannel bedroom slippers
she is sipping coffee
she is thinking—
      —gazing at the weedy bumpy yard
at the faces beginning to take shape
in the wavy mud
in the linoleum
where floorboards assert themselves

Women whose lives are food
breaking eggs with care
scraping garbage from the plates
unpacking groceries hand over hand

Wednesday evening: he takes the cans out front
tough plastic with detachable lids
Thursday morning: the garbage truck whining at 7
Friday the shopping mall open till 9
bags of groceries unpacked
hand over certain hand

Men whose lives are money
time-and-a-half Saturdays
the lunchbag folded with care and brought back home
unfolded Monday morning

Women whose lives are food
because they are not punch-carded
because they are not unclocked
sighing glad to be alone
staring into the yard, mid-morning

mid-week
by mid-afternoon everything is forgotten

There are long evenings
panel discussions on abortions, fashions, meaningful work
there are love scenes where people mouth passions
sprightly, handsome, silly, manic
in close-ups revealed ageless
the women whose lives are food
the men whose lives are money
fidget as these strangers embrace and weep and mis-
      understand and forgive and die and weep and embrace
and the viewers stare and fidget and sigh and
begin yawning around 10:30
never make it past midnight, even on Saturdays,
watching their brazen selves perform

Where are the promised revelations?
Why have they been shown so many times?
Long-limbed children a thousand miles to the west
hitch-hiking in spring, burnt bronze in summer
thumbs nagging
eyes pleading
*Give us a ride, huh? Give us a ride?*

and when they return nothing is changed
the linoleum looks older
the Hawaiian Chicken is new
the girls wash their hair more often
the boys skip over the puddles
in the GM parking lot
no one eyes them with envy

their mothers stoop
the oven doors settle with a thump
the dishes are rinsed and stacked and

by mid-morning the house is quiet
it is raining out back
or not raining
the relief of emptiness rains
simple, terrible, routine
at peace

# Ford

for Robert Phillips

If you stare long enough perhaps it becomes beautiful.
If you translate its colors into comely sounds—
ochre, russet, coppery-pink, nutmeg—
perhaps it becomes merely an anti-world,
another way of seeing.

An industrial slum gaily glaring
in a mid-summer squall:
porous smoke rising heavy and leaden-pale as a giant's limbs,
the sickly air heaving in gusts,
sulphurous blooms whipping in the wind.
Here, an ancient sea-bed
guarded by a twelve-foot chain link fence.
Clouds break companionably about the highest smokestacks.
Factory windows, opaque with grime, slant open
into the 100° shade.
You stare, you memorize, you do not wish to judge.
Your lungs shrink shy of the bold air.

Scars' stitchings in the earth,
high-tension wires whining thinly overhead.
What is there to say about what we see,
what is the compulsion to make judgments,
to invent visions?

This is the base of the pyramid, of course.
But it is not strewn with workers' bones:
it glowers and winks with their acres of parked cars.
If the air is noxious perhaps it is you who have wakened.

It is you who wonder what creatures graze in such pastures,
brood beside such rancid ponds—
giant crab-spiders of wire and rust,

toads with swollen white bellies,
armored things with spiny tails and eyes
staring unperturbed at the ends of stalks.
It is you who observes most of *Ford* obscured by filth:
And you who see again at the top of the highest smokestack
the same plastic wreath you'd seen at Christmas,
wondering if it was a joke:
*Joy to the World   Gilmore Chemicals.*

What is there to say about what we see,
what we cannot not see,
our eyes stinging helpless with tears?

## The Abandoned Altmire Mine

The skulls of miners lie scattered
like stones, tiny lineaments of coal
their eyes and lips. Beneath

rubble mountains of tailings
the secret histories of children
are worn into rock.

When the wind rises
the clean leaves whisper
like crisp dollars
riffled for show.

## The Miners at Revloc

Coal has entered their skin.
A fine black salt drifts
back into their meals.
Every day the mills are fed
tiny wafers of their flesh.

## Retired Miners

in Dr. Capelletti's office,
crippled and wheezing:

"if any guy          tells you
he got rich          through hard work
ask him              whose?"

## The World We Dreamed Of

the factories shimmer
in the pure hum of machines

a watchman slumps toward sleep
on his balustrade

we play on the choked wealth
of production through the golden corridors
of afternoons

ore from Patagonia and Durban
pours down the chutes
by itself

this is what we have dreamed of:
to be rich and not be ashamed,
to watch our daughters dance alone
down fields of the world empty
as far as our eyes can see

## Reaganomics Comes to Pittsburgh

All at once
arms, legs, hips, eyes, tongue
all at once
everything jerks skyward like inflation
pushes through the coarse blanket and lifts up
as if sensing bright stars in April black
lurking beyond the thick slate roof, beyond reach.

Quiet. Everything quiet.
My father, awake
bolt upright like rolled steel
bolt upright and sweating pellets
in the night. Quiet.
Even the sweat ribboning his back
makes no sound.

Everything at American Bridge, J. and L. Steel
quiet.
The Beaver Valley is dry, quiet.
The Ohio River sucks in on itself.
The sheen of rolled steel,
steam of river-dumped waste are no longer.
In Ambridge, Aliquippa, Baden
the roads and bridges, streets and trees
dry up and blow away leaving the dull hard sheen
of metal shavings with no footprints through them.

Awake. My father awake and sweating.
Beside him my mother watches the small glow of
cigarette ash and remembers.
Great iron cauldrons brimming hot steel
yellow-white glow in night, and sweat, and noise.
Father's great hands wrapped around the sure ring
of shovel in coal, the sure ring of the sound of steel,
and paycheck and pride.

172

Re-train and re-train is what the President says.
Good jobs, solid jobs, different fields,
re-train and re-train.
"I'm fifty-nine years old, for God's sake Mr. Reagan
fifty-nine years old. You want me to study computers
and biology now? You want me to work at McDonalds;
sixteen-year-old kids and three thirty-five an hour?"

My mother says it over breakfast
over the back fence to neighbors.
My father's eyes say it, always.
Who ever thought that steel mills would be
a thing of the past?
But they are
and it's here
all together
all alone
all at once.

## My Father

My father was four years in the war,
and afterward, according to my mother,
had nothing to say. She says he trembled
in his sleep the next four years.
My father was twice the father of sons
miscarried, and afterward, said nothing.
My mother keeps this silence also.
Four times my father was on strike,
and according to my mother, had nothing
to say. She says the company didn't understand,
nor can her son, the meaning
of an extra 15 cents an hour in 1956
to a man tending a glass furnace in August.

I have always remembered him a tired man.
I have respected him like a guest
and expected nothing.
It is April now.
My life lies before me
enticing as the woman at my side.
Now, in April, I want him to speak.
I want to stand against the worn body
of his pain. I want to try it on
like a coat that does not fit.

## The Story of Glass

From the holes of the earth, from
truck, from silo, from cullet,
from scale, batch, tank, heat-wind; from

heat, from ribbon, from flow, roll
roll, from lehr, they feed the line.

They crosscut, snap, they flour lites,
plates, plates, plates on belts, coveys,
glass, glass you grab, you pull, you

lift, you pack, you kick, you count,
and you turn, they feed the line.

You reach, you grab, you pack, you
tap, into skid, into crane,
into pack, uncut and cut-

down, they stock, they bay, they stack
skid, skid on skid, box, and they

feed the line. They multi-cut,
they Race 1, they feed you glass
and it comes, it waits, you pack,

it moves, stops, and you pack, it
comes, it comes, it comes without

pause, it comes without thought, it
comes without Jesus or Marx,
it comes, it comes, you pack, they

feed the line. You band, you crimp,
you ship to Kuwait, Detroit,

·

to Crestline, Ohio, they
profit, it comes, they feed the
line. You eat, you sleep, you bail

glass from your dreams, you drown, you
faint, you rest, you rage, you love,

feed, they feed
the line, glass, industry you,
from earth.

## Landscape with Unemployed, 1934

What we feel
has to do with the air
so sweet
it is sickening.

Has to do with the air
so clear
it is sickening.
We march arm in arm

so clear
in the street of lilies.
We march arm in arm
wearing sober hats

in the street of lilies,
singing, "No jobs! No jobs!"
wearing sober hats,
the radical priests

singing, "No jobs! No jobs!"
casting shadows,
the radical priests
who celebrate us, and sing us,

casting shadows
the color of burnt earth,
who celebrate us, and sing us,
as we lean and loaf,

the color of burnt earth.
We loaf and invite our souls.
We lean and loaf
on the summer grass,

loaf and invite our souls—
born here
on the summer grass—
hoping they'll never cease.

Born here,
we watch flames opening,
hoping they'll never cease
and we hurry along the street.

We watch flames opening
all the windows
and we hurry along the street,
our shadows sticking.

All the windows
of where we worked, burning,
our shadows sticking
to the burnt earth

of where we worked, burning.
Such shadows, Van Gogh said,
must be daubed on with a knife.
The burnt earth.

Our shadows sticking.
What we feel,
*no jobs, no jobs,*
what we feel.

## The Annual PPG Pensioners' Picnic

When I awoke it was almost dark, the sun
half sunk, silent and purple. I remember the pungent
dampness, the rot of needles, the scent of sausage
lifting me as I trudged along the path
a little woozy, a little twisted with sleep.
Look—Father Korba was dealing now and telling jokes
he had learned on retreat, but none of them in English.
My grandfather clicked his teeth.
"Come on, come on now!" he muttered,
his sandwich in one hand, his cards in the other.
For just a minute I felt pure. For maybe the first time
I felt lucid and sentimental about his straw hat,
about his white socks, about his pony bottles of beer,
his Hunky music wafting over from the grove.
I babbled at him and waved my arms and kissed him
on both cheeks. We set off for the parking lot
to consider the winter of 1913 and the fat years
after the second war. We danced a little
in the cinders, in the glow from the rim of the sky.
We watched the valley stretch
below us and the river wind away for miles and the bats
shriek and dip below the bridge.
We crossed ourselves, moaning, "God preserve us!"
under the moon rising small and thin,
as the mill fumed, as the town glimmered, as the star ignited
above it, burning like a carefully carried candle.

## After the Deindustrialization of America, My Father Enters Television Repair

My hands hold, my father's solder the wires—
picture rolls once, then steadies . . . an English castle!
The voice-over drones about Edward I,
who, to subdue the Welsh, built castles.
Some sixty years, dozens of engineers, the masses
conscripted from the villages.

My father moves on to a Zenith
with a bad tuner. TVs interest him, not the English
with their damp, historical programming.
                              •
Here there were Indians, mound builders.
Here, an English fort, a few farmers.
And here the industrialist settled his ass,
John Ford on the river dredging sand
for making glass. Plate glass.
(Why should America buy from Europe?)
Some half dozen years, German engineers, and hundreds
        of Slavic peasants.

Grandfather sat on his samovar
warming himself and making excuses,
but finally, he set off.
Got a room, became a shoveler.
Got a wife, a company house.
Ford City: a valley filling with properties.

No one got along—
not Labor and Capital, not Germans and Slavs,
not husbands and wives, for that matter.
                              •
Edward's castles were ruins
by the 15th century. Not from Welsh armies,
but the rise of the middle class.
The towns around a castle thrived:

tailors, smithies, cobblers, coopers.
Drawing in the Welsh peasants.
And what with intermarriage and the rise
        of capitalism . . .
a castle grew obsolescent.

I turn off the set. My father hunts
cigarettes at the Kwik-Mart on the corner.
Overhead, my mother's footsteps,
the tonk of bottles,
the scraping of plates.

                •

During Eisenhower's reign
my grandfather retired and mowed his lawn
until I took over. He primed the filter,
set the choke, then we took turns pulling
till the sputtering engine caught.
("Somanabitch," he'd spit.)
And watch me as I mowed
back and forth for two dollars.

Once in the garage he showed me a scythe.
He mowed hay in the old country, and the women
would follow, raking it in windrows.

                •

The factories today are mostly closed down,
or full of robots or far off in Asia.
Ford City lives through the mail:
compensation, a thin pension,
and, of course, Social Security.

I always drive along the factory, windows rolled down;
I want my kids in the back seat to see.
Seven or eight, probably pensioners, congregate
on the corner, each man dressed quite alike:
Sears jacket, cigarette, salt-and-pepper hair.

"Honk the horn," my oldest begs.
He waves and waves zealously
until a man turns—a man
with my face, but full of sweetness now,
silence and clarity.

## Toward the Heaven of Full Employment

Out of love for the dead Kennedys,
    out of fear of her laid-off spouse,
Aunt Sophie lit candles and prayed an extra rosary
    so God would make the payment on the house.

Even then factories like carriers at sea
    steamed off toward the Far East.
Even then the men, paging magazines,
    smoked more, grew bored and obese.

Mock on, mock on, Mr. Marx & Mr. Engels,
    this America of the idle and decadent.
Haul us up, slow God, speed us like angels
    toward the heaven of full employment.

## Now

Now the silence. Now the peace.
Now the empty hands uplifted. And my father, now
the pensioner, recites a psalm before
the ikon, addresses praise to the cloudy
forehead of God.
                    Now the morning, all crammed with
heaven, and the mystery of cigarettes and coffee.
Behind the cup and smoke, behind the radio's low mutter
he empties his head, turning more inward hourly.
I want said what needs said: his story wide and long now,
a public account, out of the furnace of the private life.
I want to trust it, to own it, to sit between boredom
and wonder watching it rise beneath the dome of stars, over
the tender years, over the wars, over the mill's crooked
gloom, the long arcs rising, rising toward the triumphant,
toward the end of historical time. I want his silence
broken now and what is mine.

*No,* he says, *I have no story.*
*The story tells me. Even now.*

## A Job on the Night Shift

He is the prince of tin cans
here on the nightshift.
His job is to pick up
what has fallen, to crawl
among the constant gears
beneath the conveyors
that carry the regiments
of cans, the peaches
jostling under the gloved hands
of women who joke or curse
in Spanish under the nightlong
surging of engines.
He stops and leans
on his dolly to stare
at the fluent hands of the women
as they sort the fruit.
So many peaches the hands
fly over, so many nights,
so many voices hushed
or lost, so many peaches,
so many nights, nights
that carry him south
on the road to Magdalena
where the shadows hunched
over fires in oil drums
are dead men, uncles, brothers.
And the children run
in the night streets,
coils of firecrackers
snapping at their heels.
He can almost see their faces
but the foreman touches
his shoulder and orders "move it."
So he moves it
loaded with fallen cans
out the back door of the cannery

to his station under the stars
and yellow bug lights.
His job is to salvage
what he can. He has
a tool for straightening them
and a tank of cool still water
to wash them in, a tank
of water where the yellow lights
float among the power lines
and the stars, and when he bends
to his work over the water
there is the prince of tin cans.

## Playing in the Mines

Never go down there, fathers told you,
over and over. The hexing cross
nailed onto the door read DANGER, DANGER.
But playing in the mines once every summer,
you ignored the warnings. The door
swung easier than you wished; the sunlight
followed you down the shaft a decent way.
No one behind you, not looking back,
you followed the sooty smell of coal dust,
Close damp walls with a thousand facets,
the vaulted ceiling with a crust of bats,
till the tunnel narrowed, and you came
to a point where the playing stopped.
You heard old voices pleading in the rocks;
they were all your fathers, longing to fix you
under their gaze and to go back with you.
But you said to them NEVER, NEVER,
as a chilly bile washed round your ankles.
You stood there wailing your own black fear.

## Working the Face

On his belly with a coal pick
mining underground:
the pay was better for one man
working the face.
Only one at a time could get
so close, his nose
to the anthracite, funneling
light from a helmet, chipping,
with his eyes like points of fire.
He worked, a taproot
tunneling inward, layer
by layer, digging
in a world of shadows,
thick as a slug against the floor,
dark all day long.
Wherever he turned, the facets
showered a million stars.
He was prince of darkness,
stalking the village at 6 P.M.,
having been to the end of it,
core and pith
of the world's rock belly.

## The Miner's Wake

in memoriam: E.P.

The small ones squirmed in suits and dresses,
wrapped their rosaries round the chair legs,
tapped the walls with squeaky shoes.

But their widowed mother, at thirty-four,
had mastered every pose of mourning,
plodding the sadness like an ox through mud.

Her mind ran well ahead of her heart,
making calculations of the years without him
that stretched before her like a humid summer.

The walnut coffin honeyed in sunlight;
calla lilies bloomed over silk and satin.
Nuns cried heaven into their hands

while I, a nephew with my lesser grief,
sat by a window, watching pigeons
settle onto slag like summer snow.

## Coal Train

Three times a night it woke you
in middle summer, the Erie Lackawanna,
running to the north on thin, loud rails.
You could feel it coming a long way off:
at first, a tremble in your belly,
a wire trilling in your veins, then diesel
rising to a froth beneath your skin.
You could see the cowcatcher,
wide as a mouth and eating ties,
the headlight blowing a dust of flies.
There was no way to stop it.
You lay there, fastened to the tracks
and waiting, breathing like a bull,
your fingers lit at the tips like matches.
You waited for the thunder of wheel and bone,
the axles sparking, fire in your spine.
Each passing was a kind of death,
the whistle dwindling to a ghost in air,
the engine losing itself in trees.
In a while, your heart was the loudest thing,
your bed was a pool of night.

## Anthracite Country

The culm dump burns all night,
unnaturally blue, and well below heaven.
It smolders like moments almost forgotten,
the time when you said what you meant
too plainly and ruined your chance of love.

Refusing to dwindle, fed from within
like men rejected for nothing specific,
it lingers at the edge of town, unwatched
by anyone living near. The smell now
passes for nature. It would be missed.

Rich earth-wound, glimmering
rubble of an age when men
dug marrow from the land's dark spine,
it resists all healing.
Its luminous hump cries comfortable pain.

## The Orange Bears

The orange bears with soft friendly eyes
Who played with me when I was ten,
Christ, before I left home they'd had
Their paws smashed in the rolls, their backs
Seared by hot slag, their soft trusting
Bellies kicked in, their tongues ripped
Out, and I went down through the woods
To the smelly crick with Whitman
In the Haldeman-Julius edition,
And I just sat there worrying my thumbnail
Into the cover—What did he know about
Orange bears with their coats all stunk up with soft coal
And the National Guard coming over
From Wheeling to stand in front of the millgates
With drawn bayonets jeering at the strikers?

I remember you could put daisies
On the windowsill at night and in
The morning they'd be so covered with soot
You couldn't tell what they were anymore.

A hell of a fat chance my orange bears had!

DONALD A. PETESCH

*On the Line in Oakland, California*

for Jim Daniels

"At least when I was back in Kentucky I felt like I was running
the mule. Here I feel like the mule is running me."
—Chuck, on the line

"The auto factory is a gold-plated sweatshop."
—Walter Reuther

And where is Chuck who worked down the line?
When the line stopped he leaned
against the steel like steel was home,
was a hill in Kentucky
was a freighter rolling into dock
in some port somewhere.
Chuck, school-drop-out—merchant-marine—veteran
who drove a mule in Kentucky
who explained so clearly
the mysteries of internal combustion engines
that I floated through that engine
like an electron microscope
down some artery of the human body.
Chuck who tooled through fog on the freeway
so thick the cars and trees swam past like dreams,
who said "this fog ain't nothing
when you've gone up the Thames in November,"
who only worried that his family in Kentucky
might find out: he worked with niggers.

And where am I
who forgets Chuck for whole months at a time,
who lied about my college to get the job,
who answered to "Tex" on the line,
who stared at my infant son and my daughter
in the darkness, who heard
my wife breathing in her sleep
in those hours after midnight

193

when the line shut down,
when the graveyard shift
dropped their tools like shit,
who one morning at two o'clock
standing in the kitchen with a beer in my hand
the paint dust still dry in my throat
watched the kitchen door move down the line
away from me, ran to catch it,
and stood in the middle of the floor
weeping.

## Jurgis Petraskas, the Workers' Angel, Organizes the First Miners' Strike in Exeter, Pennsylvania

Draped in khaki, Jurgis
who steals chickens
makes his way in the black dust
among the workers—so tired
and slow—trying to persuade them
that some abstraction is worth their jobs.
Jurgis with fireflies in his head.
    The old women sipping from a little bottle
of whiskey shake their heads and pray
to Matka Boza, virgin of virgins,
to deliver us from this affliction,
this crazy man who tells everyone
God is not good enough to them.
The girls don't sing on the steps anymore,
Matka Boza, and all we hear is the tune
Jurgis's troublesome bones play.
    When the sun reaches the highest place in the sky
everyone stops and eats while the good lord of the day
spreads his shadows over the dreams of his people—
the hot bodies in the mines, the streets
where nothing moves
until we stir like flies. Tomorrow
the angel of his own lord,
the weight of his passion, digs his own grave
inciting the miners to riot in Memorial Street
where the troopers kneel hunched over
their black Fords, tipped off, waiting.

## A Pennsylvania Family

### 1.

The Petraskases used to run whiskey
along with milk deliveries
during the Depression. Cows, chickens,
ducks, and goats cluttered the small yard
until the second house was built
and hard times over.

The Wyoming Valley was never rich,
except for the mines,
taking more life
than it gave. The women
held the families together.
Scrawny, rough-handed
women who could pick mushrooms
by sight, knew the feeling

of good mash and tasted
with their fingers.

Like patches of brown moss
their children grew
to the dress factories,
farms, and mines.

### 2.

Night shift, small change
in the bars, the men want to sleep:
apples, pears for a second, a century
away from slag and coal.

Old man Petraskas worked the mines
until he died and refused to let his sons
do the same. They worked the stills,
delivering what finally saved them,
the whiskey.

196

3.

I lean hard against my brain;
slowly
like a wet sack of sugar
an old lady
in a noisy green chair
rocking back and forth
calls my name:
Antanas, Antanas.

Secretly,
like sounds
pressing against the night,
I am making my way
to join her.

## Photograph

Through the rain I see huge moonless spaces,
intricate scars in the earth,
a fine thread of water.
Two voices in the clouded space name the planets,
the moon, the earth.

Postwar mining town,
the color of stone and Kodachrome
fades into the women's eyes. They're there
in Exeter, Pennsylvania, counting, chanting in Lithuanian
the names of mines and mills with the same slow song
that seeps through the dark tunnels.

So this is the way silent things speak.
Who told the stars their names?
Certainly not the man in the photograph
too long in the paper mills
where the only stars are in his swollen eyes.

There is little to be said
for that misguided winter
when my father went to work in the mills.

## Liberty Avenue

It's so hot tonight.
The boys prowling the streets
with their shirts off,
and their girls wandering aimlessly
always seem to find someone they know
on every corner. The bars are still open too,
and the smell of fried fish hangs in the humid air.
This is the kind of night I will remember Pittsburgh for—
the kids in doorways listening to radios and smoking dope,
the blond mopsticks lined-up
in the hardware store windows
like assembly line workers,
like my father, with his silver hair
and ingratiating fatalism.

## My Father Is

My father is a small man
who wears flannel shirts,
silver-blue workpants,
a matching blue billed hat,
and works on an assembly line
in a shed that stretches for acres.
All day he stands on concrete,
the noise from the machines
vibrating through him.

Years ago when my sister left,
my mother lost hold of herself.
Now she wants to leave
and my father, brooding,
won't let anyone near him.

I still do not understand.
The house closes in.
I ask about my sister,
we are strangers. My mother
cooks a big meal and we eat,
talking about the neighbors and relatives,
while my father argues with the past.

## The Visit

Almost twenty years ago Frank Pazdziorko, my uncle,
died in a mine cave-in just north of Pittston, Pennsylvania
where the Susquehanna turns yellow
while Annie hung the laundry out.
When the sirens went off, all she could see
was a cloud of black smoke.

They never got any of the bodies out of that mine.
Annie took her two daughters south.
We kept our distance
and never talked after we saw each other when grandmother died
and this was after that.
She was askew nervously picking at her fingers
while we looked through an old photograph album.

Frank used to come home drunk and slap her around.
Their voices were hard as nails,
and they were always bickering.
Once he put his fist through the bedroom door.
I was amazed.
I never believed anyone could do that.

## The Boys

The mills haven't pitted their faces yet.
On prom night they usher their girls
into the neighbors' bushes,
into their fathers' Chevrolets,
where the girls don't bother to fake
affection, innocence or climax.

It isn't all bleak. On summer nights
when the moon broils over Bethlehem Steel,
the boys get a little cooked
& stagger into pastures outside of town
where rapidly, & with much ferocity,
the boys punch the hell out of cows,
the cows dropping at their feet like statues,
the boys having one hell of a good time
planning the route back to town
where they will play bloody knuckles
against any brick wall they can find.

## Belle's Body

The miners in Morbito's Tavern
drank themselves drunk every Friday night
beneath the bump and shimmy
& jut of her grinding muscles.
She'd grease their minds blind,
rotate one tassel on one nipple
with dips of her shoulder, then
rotate the other in teasingly slow circles.

Everyone forgot his wife
& occasionally the rules of the house.
One night, when a drunk below the stage
brushed Belle's bare right foot,
two apes came snorting from behind the bar
& pounded the living shit out of him,
& everybody agreed he deserved it
because everybody knew nobody touched
Belle's body. Belle's body was the body
that came utterly naked and white
into all of their bedrooms
when the kids stopped crying
& the wife fell asleep.

## Strangers

Women at rows of seamstress tables.
Heads bent over swaths of fabric,
except at lunch or when the Portuguese cutters tease
them. My aunt's hair, and her friend's, going
gray while the dyed threads get brighter—
though one day Mary wears an auburn wig to the shop,
my aunt's slightly jealous. Through high windows
they could see a bridge. I was crossing it

on a bus, to come back to the other life.
I'd been bored to hatred by whoever
stood at the front of my high school classes,
even while I read until the print
slurred late at night. When I woke,
I'd lie there, listening to the morning noises
of our apartment, hearing them
nearly as a stranger might.
Then a few years later I left.
I could come and go as I pleased.
I'd gotten away with something.
People in Fall River believe the days,

like huge boxes, get filled up by work.
Now, through the grimy bus windows,
I was watching painters
with air guns crawl the girders of the bridge.
My mother was probably leaving her desk
at the bank, the fluorescent lamps,
walking out onto the street, as distracted and glad
as a woman in a novel
standing in a warm garden. The painters were coating
the bridge a silver-white color,
and for a moment it was swallowed by fog, the tenacious
diffuse sky.

## Torque

After his ham & cheese in the drape factory cafeteria,
having slipped by the bald shipping foreman
to ride a rattling elevator to the attic
where doves flicker into the massive eaves
and where piled boxes of out-of-style
cotton and lace won't ever be
decorating anyone's sun-parlor windows.
Having dozed off in that hideout he fixed
between five four-by-six cardboard storage cartons
while the rest of us pack Mediterranean Dreams
and Colonial Ruffles and drapes colored like moons,
and he wakes lost—
shot through
into a world of unlocked unlocking light—
suddenly he knows where he is and feels half-nuts
and feels like killing some pigeons with a slingshot.

That's all, and that's why he pokes
his calloused fingers into the broke machinery,
hunting for loose nuts a half-inch wide—
five greasy cold ones that warm in his pocket—
and yanks back the snag-cut strip of inner tube
with a nut snug at the curve to snap it
at the soft chest of a dopey bird.
Then the noise of pigeons flopping down
to creosoted hardwood, and then a grin
the guy gives me & all his other pals later.
And afternoon tightens down on all
our shoulders, until shift whistle finally
blows & fills the air like sunlight
through lace. As it always has, as it does.
That bright. That stunned.

## Coal Miners

I wake from a dream of coal miners
in Cohoes turning into glittering pieces
of coal, burning, hands and faces on fire, and
in this north light of a cold room I shiver, feel
the wind move through me as it blows into
their ashes; I know we are in this together.

No wonder I don't care the day is breaking
in half while I can still see the copper light
in the coal tunnel of dream, the miners' bodies
burning in the dark seams, and I think
this is not hell, but heaven, light
arms and chests, translucent hands
and sapphire necks, each one touching
off the other until there is nothing left.

## At the Train Tracks

Another springtime, another dollar. I wonder
as I drive from one job to another
how many more hours, honest-to-God alive
hours I have left, how many more Christmasses
I will buy the unnecessary gifts, how many more
summers limit myself to two weeks vacation on a lake
when that's all I'd like to do with my life.
Held up at the tracks I watch the B & O line,
the L & N, the Lackawanna, the Reading, the rusted metal
wheels clickety-clacking like mad days
on the shining steel while behind me automobiles
pile up, one driver blowing his horn
as though there were some other way across.

## Aunt Dolly

Sitting there on the
assembly line piecing
together frocks all alike
thousands by thousands, for
millions to buy, the same
cheap pattern duplicated
all over the world, goes
home at night and sews
up a storm, a dream that
nobody has "ever" seen
who can deny, when "ever"
she steps out the door,
any day or hour, after work,
after five, she is a *queen*.
She can sew anything you
cannot even imagine.

## Alone with the Shoe Manufacturer in His Memorial Park

You bang on the statue's metal knee
and speed off, chasing around the square.
You think you're such a flash
with your red shirt flapping in the breeze.
Then you are long gone and I'm alone
with George F. Johnson, his calm hand
clenched against one ringing, greenish knee.
I stroke the cold wrist of industrial man,
a chill straight through the finger bone.
One docile boy and girl kneel at his side
in shoes no mother's love could bronze so huge.
And four feet down a thickly muscled man of iron broods
on his mystical code: *Labor is Honorable*.

Here are the first uncertainties
of spring, but nothing comforts me,
gone stiff with terror, surrounded by the dead
and silent birds sleeping in the trees.
I find dark hieroglyphs on the girl's lace hem.
*Have faith in the people*. But where are they?
The iron boy studies his anchored shoe.
Some stranger runs maniacally at me,
mouth open in wind, hair like a nimbus
lit by the greasy streetlamp glare.
I grab at his cool, familiar hand, the streak
of red life leaping through the shadowy park.

## The Furniture Factory

Upstairs the sanders
rubbed fingernails
thin, hands shiny
and soft as a barber's—
men past forty
down on their luck.
Below, I worked in a haze
of fine dust
sifting down—
the lives of the sanders
sifting down, delicately
riding the cluttered
beams of light.
I pounded nails
on the line.
The wood swallowed hard
nailheads like coins
too thin to pick up.
Lunchtimes I read—
You gonna be
a lawyer, Ace?—
then forgot the alphabet
as I hammered
afternoons flat.
My father worked there too
breathing the sanding
room's haze.
We ate quiet lunches together
in the car.
In July
he quit—hands
soft, thick fingernails
feathery at the tips.

## The Ditch

In the ditch, half-ton sections of cast-iron molds
hand-greased at the seams with pale petroleum waste
and screw-clamped into five-hundred-gallon cylinders
drummed with rubber-headed sledges inside and out
to settle tight the wet concrete
that, dried and caulked, became Monarch Septic Tanks;
and, across the ditch, my high school football coach,
Don Compo, spunky pug of a man,
bronze and bald, all biceps and pecs,
raging at some "attitude" of mine
he snipped from our argument about Vietnam—
I mean *raging*, scarlet, veins bulging from his neck,
he looked like a hard-on stalking back and forth—
but I had started college, this was a summer job,
I no longer had to take his self-righteous, hectoring shit,
so I was chuckling merrily, saying he was ludicrous,
and he was calling me "College Man Ryan"
and with his steel-toed workboot kicking dirt
that clattered against the molds and puffed up between us.

It's probably not like this anymore, but every coach
in my hometown was a lunatic. Each had different quirks
we mimicked, beloved bromides whose parodies we intoned,
but they all conducted practice like bootcamp,
the same tirades and abuse, no matter the sport,
the next game the next battle in a neverending war.
Ex-paratroopers and -frogmen, at least three
finally-convicted child molesters, genuine sadists
fixated on the Commie menace and our American softness
that was personally bringing the country to the brink of collapse—
in this company, Don Compo didn't even seem crazy.
He had never touched any of us;
his violence was verbal, which we were used to,
having gotten it from our fathers
and given it back to our brothers and to one another
since we had been old enough to button our own pants.

Any minute—no guessing what might spring it—
he could be butting your face-mask and barking up your nostrils,
but generally he favored an unruffled, moralistic carping
in which I, happy to spot phoniness,
saw pride and bitterness masquerading as teaching.
In the locker-room, I'd sit where I could roll my eyeballs
as he droned, but, across the ditch,
he wasn't lecturing, but fuming, flaring
as I had never seen in four years of football,
and it scared and thrilled me to defy him and mock him
when he couldn't make me handwash jockstraps after practice
or do pushups on my fingertips in a mud puddle.

But it was myself I was taunting. I could see my retorts
snowballing toward his threat to leap the ditch
and beat me to a puddle of piss ("you craphead,
you wiseass"), and my unspading a shovel from a dirt pile
and grasping its balance deliberately down the handle
and inviting him to try it.
Had he come I would have hit him.
There's no question about that.
For a moment, it ripped through our bewilderment,
which then closed over again
like the ocean
if a cast-iron mold were dropped in.
I was fired when the boss broke the tableau.
"The rest of you," he said, "have work to do,"
and, grabbing a hammer and chisel, Don Compo
mounted the mold between us in the ditch
and with one short punch split it down the seam.

## Motown

The rock star
rising
the hard way,
from an auto workers'
neighborhood in Detroit,
playing the beer halls
the grass and acid alleys
of the Great Lakes,
the Ohio Valley,
singing
the grungy
neighborhood of Detroit

got a smash hit

a gold record

turned this
disc
into a Corvette,
a river cruiser,
a platinum record,
invested this
in shares
of GM,
cashing in
again
on the 1st 2nd 3rd shift
the office drudges
kitchens and kids
of that
neighborhood in Detroit

where his fame
persists,
clings to the street

like confetti
after a wedding,
after the wedding
party has driven off.

## Enough!

And now they are no longer
man and father,
woman and mother,
but 2
workers in old age:
heroic and used up
as smoldering rags.

Her, she's
a tiny cell of light
—40 watts, say,
against 3 backyards
and one small, dirty sidestreet—
in an immense night.

She dreams no more
than the dog, Toro,
chained to the back porch.

Six days she goes
out in the marbled mist
of streetlamps, dawn, dripping trees,
the sky
with its wisp of moon.

Sundays she sleeps.

Across the city, by the harbor,
the cable coiling
machines she tends
are not what they are,
but the oily roar
of her horizon.
An end.

And him?
Back from the hospital
he sits in the kitchen.
His brain scatters
wishes
and insights, like fireflies
through the terrible spring night

only to say
how dark it is,

how 38 years
boxing chemicals and beakers,
grinding glass,
add up
to $57.60 each month
for life: enough
for dog food, cheap
stupefying wine,
rest beyond belief.

It is more
than enough.

## Mission Tire Factory, 1969

All through lunch Peter pinched at his crotch,
And Jesus talked about his tattoos,
And I let the flies crawl my arm, undisturbed,
Thinking it was wrong, a buck sixty-five,
The wash of rubber in our lungs,
The oven we would enter, squinting
—because earlier in the day Manny fell
From his machine, and when we carried him
To the workshed (blood from
Under his shirt, in his pants)
All he could manage, in an ignorance
Outdone only by pain, was to take three dollars
From his wallet, and say:
"Buy some sandwiches. You guys saved my life."

## The Miners of Delta

In the anonymous night I see them,
in the shadows thrown on the house
by the random shouts of dogs and sirens,
in the breath of cars that rise and fall
on the wind and the radio beam's
slow cut through the roofs.
In the silhouette of the boy next door,
monstrous in the cap pistol's light,
and in my own eyes caught
between the window and the screen,
unable to turn toward the night, I
see them carrying their picks and
torches through the empty streets
of Delta; they are pulling
the stubborn quarry behind them
into the shattered light, into morning.

Everywhere they haunt the day,
in the checkout line at the supermarket,
and the lines at the movies and stations,
in the far seats of the subway
and the booths at the back
of the diner; everywhere the Delta
miners, silently watching
the living, drifting between
the slate's dull faces
that have somehow been broken into sky;
through the blue of the Susquehanna
and the marbled veins of their arms,
through the blue of their shirts
and their shoes and the heaving
blue of their lungs, they walk
with their twine linked around
their waists, their voices held
together by the heavy hymns of Wales.
In the drum of childhood bedrooms

and the startled voice of my husband
in his sleep, in the wall's electric hum
and the radiator rattling against the
dark, I hear their hammers and hatchets,
ringing the hours on the sides of the quarry,
blinding the water's eye below them
with the dust and smoke of their hands.
Here in the blanket's folds
are the bodies made of peat
and sandbags, here in the brooms
and the mops are the axes and chisels
of sadness; here are the Delta miners,
their faces chalked on the blackboard
night, chipping away through their own
throats and chests where their hearts
stand naked as diamonds or stars.

## The Miracle-Factory

Papa's got a job in a miracle-factory
downtown someplace, one of those streets
west of the avenue, in an old
building taller than God. There's a marble lobby, two
elevators behind brass gates, a newsstand,
and a draft whenever anyone pushes through
the glass revolving doors. Upstairs
after the corridor, damp, windy, cold
RING BELL COME IN the loft
looks like an airshaft. Soot settles softly, like snow.

I went there once with Papa. Standing soldierly
put out my hand to the boss, said, How d'you do.
I didn't like it much. The boss said, Boy,
when you grow up I want you to remember
making miracles is just like any other line, profit and loss,
also supply and demand. You got to sell
the product, make them believe
in it! He shook my hand.
Papa said later, He's the boss, without
the boss, no factory. Remember that.

## A Valedictory to Standard Oil of Indiana

In the darkness east of Chicago, the sky burns over the plumber's
    nightmares
Red and blue, and my hometown lies there loaded with gasoline.
Registers ring like gas-pumps, pumps like pinballs, pinballs like broken
    alarm clocks,
And it's time for morning, but nothing's going to work.
From cat-cracker to candle-shop, from grease-works along the pipeline,
Over storage tanks like kings on a checkerboard ready to jump the
    country,
The word goes out: With refined regrets
We suggest you sleep all day in your houses shaped like lunch buckets
And don't show up at the automated gates.
Something else will tap the gauges without yawning
And check the valves at the feet of the cooling-towers without
    complaining.
Standard Oil is canning my high school classmates
And the ones who fell out of junior high or slipped in the grades
What should they do, gassed up in their Tempests and Comets, raring
    to go
Somewhere with their wives scowling in front and kids stuffed in the
    back,
Past drive-ins jammed like car-lots, trying to find the beaches
But blocked by freights for hours, stopped dead in their tracks
Where the rails, as thick as thieves along the lakefront,
Lower their crossing gates to shut the frontier? What can they think
    about
As they stare at the sides of boxcars for a sign,
And Lake Michigan drains slowly into Lake Huron,
The mills level the Dunes, and the eels go sailing through the trout,
And mosquitoes inherit the evening, while toads no bigger than
    horseflies
Hop crazily after them over the lawns and sidewalks, and the rainbows
    fall
Flat in the oil they came from? There are two towns now,
One dark, one going to be dark, divided by cyclone fences;
One pampered and cared for like pillboxes and cathedrals,

221

The other vanishing overnight in the dumps and swamps like a struck
    sideshow.
As the Laureate of the Class of '44—which doesn't know it has one—
I offer this poem, not from hustings or barricades
Or the rickety stage where George Rogers Clark stood glued to the wall,
But from another way out, like Barnum's "This Way to the Egress,"
Which moved the suckers when they'd seen enough. Get out of town.

## Their Bodies

to the students of anatomy at Indiana University

That gaunt old man came first, his hair as white
As your scoured tables. Maybe you'll recollect him
By the scars of steel-mill burns on the backs of his hands,
On the nape of his neck, on his arms and sinewy legs,
And her by the enduring innocence
Of her face, as open to all of you in death
As it would have been in life: she would memorize
Your names and ages and pastimes and hometowns
If she could, but she can't now, so remember her.

They believed in doctors, listened to their advice,
And followed it faithfully. You should treat them
One last time as they would have treated you.
They had been kind to others all their lives
And believed in being useful. Remember somewhere
Their son is trying hard to believe you'll learn
As much as possible from them, as *he* did,
And will do your best to learn politely and truly.

They gave away the gift of those useful bodies
Against his wish. (They had their own ways
Of doing everything, always.) If you're not certain
Which ones are theirs, be gentle to everybody.

## In the Dress Factory

We unrolled the bolts of material.
Harry worked faster than the rest,
fascinated with the language of color:
*Cranberry,* he said. *Cranberry.* And
*Mahogany, Chartreuse, Cerulean.*

Louie Prince, his nose blown out
by acne, would talk about his wife
and their hot nights. He knew
the virtues of Westinghouse fans,
the intricacies of condoms,
the sensuousness of sweat
in the close St. Louis summers.

And there was Al, who could not
cut a straight line, who liked
to drop his pants for the women,
"adjusting his jock," and fondling
the bolts of material.

Meanwhile, the women,
hunched up like scraps of cloth,
sat in the corners tying knots
and sewing, their lips buttoned shut,
their quick eyes sewn in place,
only their fingers flitting
in the still dark.

So I spent the summer with them,
unrolling those long, hot days
on the table, learning from the men
how to cut things off,
learning from the women
how to sew things up, how to
tie things all together.

TOM WAYMAN

## Unemployment

The chrome lid of the coffee pot
twists off, and the glass knob rinsed.
Lift out the assembly, dump
the grounds out. Wash the pot and
fill with water, put everything back with
fresh grounds and snap the top down.
Plug in again and wait.

Unemployment is also
a great snow deep around the house
choking the street, and the City.
Nothing moves. Newspaper photographs
show the traffic backed up for miles.
Going out to shovel the walk
I think how in a few days the sun will clear this.
No one will know I worked here.

This is like whatever I do.
How strange that so magnificent a thing as a body
with its twinges, its aches
should have all that chemistry, that bulk
the intricate electrical brain
subjected to something as tiny
as buying a postage stamp.
Or selling it.

Or waiting.

## *Wayman in the Workforce:*
## *Actively Seeking Employment*

Everybody was very nice. Each place Wayman went
the receptionist said: "Certainly we are hiring.
Just fill out one of these forms." Then, silence.
Wayman would call back each plant and corporation
and his telephone would explain: "Well, you see,
we do our hiring pretty much at random. Our interviewers
draw someone out of the stack of applications we have on file.
There's no telling when you might be notified: could be next week
or the week after that. Or, you might never hear from us at all."

One Thursday afternoon, Wayman's luck ran out.
He had just completed a form for a motor truck
manufacturing establishment, handed it in to the switchboard operator
and was headed happily out. "Just a minute, sir," the girl said.
"Please take a seat over there. Someone will see you about this."

Wayman's heart sank. He heard her dialing Personnel.
"There's a guy here willing to work full time
and he says he'll do anything," she said excitedly.
Around the corner strode a man in a suit. "Want a job, eh?" he said.
He initialed one corner of the application and left.
Then a man in a white coat appeared. "I'm Gerry," the newcomer said.
"This way." And he was gone through a doorway into the plant.

"We make seven trucks a day," Gerry shouted
standing sure-footedly amid a clanking, howling, bustling din.
"Over here is the cab shop, where you'll work. I'll be your foreman.
And here is the chassis assembly . . ." a speeding forklift narrowly
    missed them
". . . and this is where we make the parts."
"Wait a minute," Wayman protested, his voice barely audible
above the roar of hammers, drills, and the rivet guns. "I'm pretty green
at this sort of thing."
                    "Nothing to worry about," Gerry said.
"Can you start tomorrow? Monday? Okay,

you enter through this door. I'll meet you here."
They were standing near an office marked *First Aid*.
"We have to do a minor physical on you now," Gerry said.
"Just step inside. I'll see you Monday."

Wayman went shakily in through the First Aid office doors.
"I need your medical history," the attendant said
as Wayman explained who he was. "Stand over here.
Thank you. Now drop your pants."
Wayman did as he was told. "You seem sort of nervous to me,"
the aid man said, as he wrote down notes to himself.
"Me, I'm a bit of an amateur psychologist. There are five hundred men
in this plant, and I know 'em all.
Got to, in my job. You shouldn't be nervous.
Remember when you apply for work you're really selling yourself.
Be bold. Where are you placed? Cab shop?
Nothing to worry about working there: monkey see, monkey do."

Then Wayman was pronounced fit, and the aid man escorted him
back through the roaring maze into the calm offices of Personnel.
There Wayman had to sign for time cards, employee number, health
    scheme
and only just managed to decline
company credit union, company insurance plan, and a company social
    club.
At last he was released, and found himself back on the street
clutching his new company parking lot sticker in a light rain.
Even in his slightly dazed condition,
a weekend away from actually starting work, Wayman could tell
he had just been hired.

## Factory Time

The day divides neatly into four parts
marked off by the breaks. The first quarter
is a full two hours, 7:30 to 9:30, but that's okay
in theory, because I'm supposed to be fresh, but in fact
after some evenings it's a long first two hours.
Then, a ten-minute break. Which is good
another way, too: the second quarter
thus has ten minutes knocked off, 9:40 to 11:30
which is only 110 minutes, or
to put it another way, if I look at my watch
and it says 11:10
I can cheer up because if I had still been in the first quarter
and had worked for 90 minutes there would be
30 minutes to go, but now there is only
20. If it had been the first quarter, I could expect
the same feeling at 9 o'clock as here I have
when it is already ten minutes after 11.

Then it's lunch: a stretch, and maybe a little walk around.
And at 12 sharp the endless quarter begins:
a full two afternoon hours. And it's only the start
of the afternoon. Nothing to hope for the whole time.
Come to think of it, today
is probably only Tuesday. Or worse, Monday,
with the week barely begun and the day
only just half over, four hours down
and 36 to go this week
(if the foreman doesn't come padding by about 3
some afternoon and ask us all to work overtime.)

Now while I'm trying to get through this early Tuesday afternoon
maybe this is a good place to say
Wednesday, Thursday and Friday have their personalities too.
As a matter of fact, Wednesday after lunch
I could be almost happy
because when that 12 noon hooter blast goes

the week is precisely and officially half over.
All downhill from here: Thursday, as you know
is the day before Friday
which means a little celebrating Thursday night
—perhaps a few rounds in the pub after supper—
won't do me any harm. If I don't get much sleep
Thursday night, so what? I can sleep in Saturday.
And Friday right after lunch Mike the foreman appears
with the long checks dripping out of his hands
and he is so polite to each of us as he passes them over
just like they taught him in foreman school.
After that, not too much gets done.
People go away into a corner and add and subtract like crazy
trying to catch the Company in a mistake
or figuring out what incredible percentage the government
has taken this week, or what the money will actually mean
in terms of savings or payments—and me, too.

But wait. It's still Tuesday afternoon.
And only the first half of that: all the minutes
until 2—which comes at last
and everyone drops what they are doing
if they hadn't already been drifting toward
their lunchboxes, or edging between the parts-racks
in the direction of the caterer's carts
which always appear a few minutes before the hooter
and may be taken on good authority as incontrovertible proof
that 2 o'clock is actually going to arrive.

And this last ten minute break of the day
is when I finally empty my lunchbox and the thermos inside
and put the now lightweight container back on its shelf
and dive into the day's fourth quarter: only 110 minutes.
Also, 20 to 30 minutes before the end I stop
and push a broom around, or just fiddle with something
or maybe fill up various parts-trays with washers

and bolts, or talk to the partsman, climb out of my
coveralls, and generally slack off.
Until the 4 P.M. hooter of hooters
when I dash to the timeclock, a little shoving and pushing
in line, and I'm done. Whew.

But even when I quit
the numbers of the minutes and hours from this shift
stick with me: I can look at a clock some morning
months afterwards, and see it is 20 minutes to 9
—that is, if I'm ever out of bed that early—
and the automatic computer in my head
starts to type out: *20 minutes to 9, that means*
*30 minutes to work after 9: you are*
*50 minutes from the break; 50 minutes*
*of work, and it is only morning, and it is only*
*Monday, you poor dumb bastard. . . .*

And that's how it goes, round the clock, until a new time
from another job bores its way into my brain.

## Tool Fondle

After some months, I take out my toolbox
and open it. Under the lid
is the tray, jammed with so many metal shapes
nestled together: my box-end wrenches of various sizes,
my ratchet and the necessary sockets
plus an extension bar, and one deep 7/16ths socket,
a cold chisel, a drift, a center punch, pliers,
and a device Bill MacKay made for me: a Phillips head
from a power screwdriver mounted into a small angled brace,
useful for attaching a hood stop cable to its mount on an engine block.

These are of dull or silvery metal. Then there are colors:
the yellow plastic handles of my assorted screwdrivers,
the deep luminous blue of the 3/8ths nutdriver handle.
A dirty cream case for my Lufkin measuring tape. An orange
cardboard package of Swedish ear cotton.
And tucked into the socket section of the tray:
some white Band-Aids, a few sticks of spearmint gum,
a pencil, red-and-white union button
and a black felt marker pen.

Slipped between the tray and the back of the toolbox
is a blank perforated time card
and above that, taped to the inside of the box lid,
are notes to myself: how to attach wear plates,
the dimensions of the aircleaner cutout
on a 736 metal hood blank (wrong, according to Jim Pope)
and finally some numbers to account for time spent
at unitglass trim, fender trim (for the hours
we were sent up to cab trim when they were behind)
and also the clean-up number which is useful every day.

Then, lifting out the heavy tray, underneath
in the bottom of the box are my gloves, a hacksaw,
a wire stripper, right- and left-hand metal shears (new)
and an old coil of twine handy for tying back a fiberglass hood

on a truck, to keep the grille from resting on the bumper
if you have to stand inside and it's short a stop cable.
Also my wooden-handled hefty ball-peen
hammer, with the wood taped where it joins the head
just in case. And one of the little yellow cardboard hood tags
useful for writing things down on.

And with all these, I built more than a thousand trucks.
Eight trucks a day for eight months:
not me alone, of course, but pulling these out
and putting them away each day
and sometimes lugging the whole heavy lot
here and there in the plant (along with about
four hundred other people similarly wandering around
and working) more than a thousand trucks at the end of Final Line
got started up, belching black smoke, or else didn't do anything
and had to be towed out into the yard
but at least were assembled.

And my grey metal toolbox used to sit every day
on a shelf next to Andy's, which was larger
as is only fitting, since he was there ten years before me
having built maybe twelve thousand trucks (allowing for the years
when lots less than eight were made each day.) And my box
was larger than Ernie's, who hardly had any tools
and was there only five months before he left,
borrowing from my box as he wanted something
the way I borrowed from Andy's at the start
and even later, if there was something Andy had that I needed
—a small bucking block, for example.

But one day, like Ernie, I closed my lid as usual
and then picked the box up (surprised once more
at the weight of all that metal)
and left for good, leaving Andy's box
still there, ready to be opened again Monday

morning, to go on building trucks
while mine
came home to a closet, where it sits
in the dark—except when I open it
for a few domestic repairs, or when a friend
wants to borrow a certain tool to work on a car.

And across the room from the closet
I've gone back to writing things down
on a typewriter, for a while
(and lots less than eight a day, too).
But every so often I get out my tools
for no good reason and stare at them.

I always meant to get a good visegrip
and a file. Maybe I'll go downtown tomorrow
and see what they're asking.

## Bosses

after Nicanor Parra

The boss who stands behind you
watching you work.
The boss who insists
"I'm sure I told you to do that."
The boss who, after you've made nine trips
carrying an extra-heavy load of boards,
sees you walking with a light load
and tells your foreman to order you to work harder.
The boss who commands you to look busy.

The foreman who can't resist showing you a better way.
The foreman who won't let you
do something a better way.
The one who is also head
of the union's grievance committee.
The foreman who is unable or forgot to
requisition enough parts
and orders you to "make do with what you have."

The supervisor who is afraid
of the boss.
The supervisor in love with memos.
The supervisor who checks the washroom
to be certain no one is there too long.
The new supervisor who doesn't understand what is happening
and so concentrates on enforcing regulations
everybody forgot about years ago.

These bosses
in their coats and ties
with their specially colored hard hats, their offices,
watches, clipboards,

with their ulcers
and their pathetic attempts to appear calm
are, by and large,
totally useless.

## The Country of Everyday:
## Literary Criticism

"He was in a hurry," Wood said, "the young foreman
only 26, down on his knees at the base of
the heavy lamppost, impatient to push it back on the block.
He was yelling at the rest of us to give him a hand
and didn't see the top of the pole, as it
swayed over and touched the powerline.

"I was looking right at him. There was a flash
and he just folded over onto his side and
turned black: his ears melted.
There were two holes burned in the pavement
where his knees were. Somebody started giving him
mouth-to-mouth and I said *Forget it. I mean, he's dead.*"

And there are poets who can enter in
to the heart of a door, and discover the rat inside us
that must be kept caged in the head because it is perfectly sane.

There are poets who claim to know what it's like
to have a crucifix wedged in the throat
unable to swallow, and how the knot of the stomach
turns into a bowl of fire.

But around and ahead of them
is the housewife endlessly washing
linoleum, sheets, fruit dishes, her hands
and the face of a child. And there is the girl who stands
in the cannery line twelve hours in season
to cut out the tips of the fish.
For the paper they tear out to write on
is pulled from the weeks of working graveyard
and all the weariness of millwork, the fatigue
of keeping it going, the urge to reclaim the body
for the hours not working or sleeping
when the body ends too tired for much but a beer and a laugh.

Beside every dazzling image, each line
desperate to search the unconscious
are the thousand hours someone is spending
watching ordinary television.
For every poet who considers the rhythm
of the word "dark" and the word "darkness"
a crew is balancing high on the grid
of a new warehouse roof, gingerly taking the first load of lumber
hauled thirty feet up to them.

For every hour someone reads critical articles
Swede is drunk in a bar again
describing how he caught his sleeve once in the winch of an oil rig
whirling him round till his ribs broke.
And for every rejection of a manuscript
a young apprentice is riding up on the crane
to work his first day on high steel.
"Left my fingerprints in the metal
when I had to grab a beam to get off," he says.
And Ed Shaw stands looking down into the hold
where a cable sprang loose lifting a pallet
and lashed across the dock, just touching one of the crew
whose body they are starting to bring up from the water.

When the poet goes out for a walk in the dusk
listening to his feet on the concrete, pondering
all of the adjectives for rain, he is walking on work
of another kind, and on lives that wear down like cement.
Somewhere a man is saying, "Worked twenty years for the City
but I'm retired now."
Sitting alone in a room, in the poorhouse of a pension
he has never read a modern poem.

## Industrial Music

for Michael Millar, Michael Taylor, Gary Walsh

After a hundred years they paused
and they heard
music; other things were on the wind
but they heard a music filling in the continent behind them:
their own music, which grew slowly,
starting at the quietest moments
like a flower, or at prayer, and at
work, and then beginning to be pumped through
cash registers, radios, and finally even leaked in
through small grilles in elevators.

But as fast as the melodies get smoothed
into a dollar, a man stands up in a noisy bar and
begins to sing, and another man joins him and
another, until the air is filled again with music,
human voices. And twenty thousand of us
are put in a single vast room
to hear one famous voice with a song rise through amplifiers
and the songs also come from just Bob Garrison
driving his '55 Willys up the Canyon from Siska
on a rainy Saturday and only me and one other
jammed into his front seat listen.

And I remember in the truck factory Boris Hukaluk drumming
everywhere, standing in Cab Electrical
tapping out the intricate rhythms with his wire stripper
and a screwdriver, but Boris also
knows everything about Folding Hoods after years
working at that before, so he gets assigned back on the days
Hoskins doesn't show. And I asked him there
why he didn't ever become a professional musician and he said
*I didn't like the life; too many late nights all the time*
so he drums weekends in a cabaret, in the house band

without even a name, and does special jobs at New Year's and
drums through his days and years at the factory
his fingers and pencils falling on the metal. One day
we are up at Test fitting a hood and one of the mechanics
picks up Boris' rhythm and sends it back to him
with his wrenches, as best he can, and Boris
grins and stops what he's doing and gives out
another short riff, and this time
a couple of guys try to match him, and Boris laughs
and taps out another complicated run
and this time maybe half a dozen guys start
clumsily pounding away after his lead. And this makes so much noise
(since somebody is banging on a waste can) that the foreman
comes out of his office to find out what's up
but sees Boris and shakes his head and goes back.

Then it's lunch and someone turns a truck radio on, and the music,
rock now, pours into the echoing Test bays
like the wind when somebody rolls aside one of the huge doors
on a cold wet February morning, the wind
flowing in off the river among the parked tires and motors,
the tool boxes, air hoses and containers of oil,
a wind that carries with it all the sounds of the City at work
this day: grudgingly, but alive, and moving.

## Machines

Most beautiful when they're turned off,
with scales of dirt on them, with our lives
all over them—derricks
hanging over the Passaic River
at rest in the smoke-dimmed sun
like rust colored washerwomen . . .
the light clean airplanes parked at Teterboro
aimed at a speck of sky to disappear in . . .
the white-decked grain ships at Welland Canal
rising or falling in the locks . . .

They make me realize something beautiful about *us*
we're going to die for. I want to forget
missiles sweating in their silos,
the poisons near Niagara, the scream of mills.
I think of men in the backwoods
of Putnam County—how crushed and lined they are
after only a few years—
how they love rifles, outboard engines,
can openers, old pickup trucks . . .
extensions of us, carnal and beautiful
things we'll die for.

## Endako Shutdown, 1982

Now they wait
bunched in the hotel coffee-shop
There is nothing to say,
the mine is closed and there is no work
Nothing to do but wait
Maybe in the new year

They were caught suddenly, incredulous
a breath stopped in mid-sentence
"This is dangerous," a man says
but even he is unsure of what he means

Dangerous for who?
The millwrights, the mechanics, the drivers,
everyone had a certain power
to make wheels turn, to start a crusher
and make it work, feel the power in it,
in themselves
Now the mine is gone, inexplicable
the hands still reach out in dreams
for levers and tools
They wake confused, not understanding
After all these years
poured into the ground
the company owes nothing
What can you put back, if money
is not enough,
when there is nowhere else to go?

All around them the machines
have stopped seized by economics
the business of men a thousand miles away
Maybe in the new year, the company says
This is what they bring home to their families,
a piece of paper crumpled in a pocket

The man in the cafe repeats,
"This is dangerous,"
his huge hands around a coffee cup
But the sentence stops, incomplete
No one is sure what he means

# Metal

for Bud

Ten years in the factory
The stacks of aluminum hung
above him, silver clouds that brought
no rain, only tumbled edges,
raw metal in the arms of a forklift
The young men from the Sally Ann
arrived for a week's work
drag hangovers to the sooty lunchroom,
the black sweat of metal dust
They pass through him
faceless as trains,
as the solemn days

Ten years, he dragged his paycheque
to the Shamrock Hotel for beer,
his room above the restaurant
The drunks howled in the tipped street,
the hookers stood like sentries on the corner
Each night in the hollow rooms,
each day in the racket of metal
he waited for something
he couldn't name

Finally, it happened
The stacks fell in the narrow aisle,
a boy caught between them
clawed by sharp angles of metal
The years collapsed in him suddenly
He drove a forklift through the lunchroom wall
Coins spilling, he speared the coke machine,
rammed its twisted slogans
across the floor and out onto the road

For the young man twisted in the fallen metal,
for the young man himself
He drove across the pot-holed Industrial Park
laughing
only the flat sky above him,
headed for the Shamrock

## Song, Endako

All the young men thrown from cars,
the bad boys drunk outside dance halls
Small town girlfriends
snuggling up close in the front seat
and only the black night highway
to pull apart finally
with the song of cylinders
and gasoline

The trip to the mine made
once too often
Raymond kept his foot on the gas pedal
left the ridge
and rose like a phoenix over the forest,
the trees singed and broken
in the fire of his loathing
His need, a spark struck against
the idiocy of everything,
the days gone mad with booze and work

Still the ore in the mine pulls
from the shovel's claw, tires howl
on the road that hugs
the torn mountain ridge

In the forest
the smell of burnt rubber mingles
with the sulphur from the mine stack
Bad boys drunk on the highway

Everyone here sings
to the stroke of engines

## Fairview Floats

Morning begins slowly here
A yawn of light stretches out of the mountains
and creeps like a stain across the sky
Fishing boats bump against the dock
as a knot of men wait, hands in pockets
in the smell of fish and gasoline

The asphalt highway drops, exhausted
into the damp cold of Prince Rupert
As so many others have arrived
looking for work
They follow the highway and the shut-down mills
to the edge of the ocean,
where the last hopes are
a few fishing boats still going out,
the rumour of a government project

Like the morning,
they have been everywhere else first
They arrive tired and hungry,
men who have never been on a boat
ask for jobs they know they won't get
Holding their pride
like a last dull coin
in the deep fold of a pocket

Grey light climbs the rocky shoreline
as the men stamp their feet and cough,
their faces grim and determined
This is the end of the road
and they will not go back

## Autumn Begins in Martins Ferry, Ohio

In the Shreve High football stadium,
I think of Polacks nursing long beers in Tiltonsville,
And gray faces of Negroes in the blast furnace at Benwood,
And the ruptured night watchman of Wheeling Steel,
Dreaming of heroes.

All the proud fathers are ashamed to go home.
Their women cluck like starved pullets,
Dying for love.

Therefore,
Their sons grow suicidally beautiful
At the beginning of October,
And gallop terribly against each other's bodies.

# Youth

Strange bird,
His song remains secret.
He worked too hard to read books.
He never heard how Sherwood Anderson
Got out of it, and fled to Chicago, furious to free himself
From his hatred of factories.
My father toiled fifty years
At Hazel-Atlas Glass,
Caught among girders that smash the kneecaps
Of dumb honyaks.
Did he shudder with hatred in the cold shadow of grease?
Maybe. But my brother and I do know
He came home as quiet as the evening.

He will be getting dark, soon,
And loom through new snow.
I know his ghost will drift home
To the Ohio River, and sit down, alone,
Whittling a root.
He will say nothing.
The waters flow past, older, younger
Than he is, or I am.

## Honey

My father died at the age of eighty. One of the last things he did in his life was to call his fifty-eight-year-old son-in-law "honey." One afternoon in the early 1930's, when I bloodied my head by pitching over a wall at the bottom of a hill and believed that the mere sight of my own blood was the tragic meaning of life, I heard my father offer to murder his future son-in-law. His son-in-law is my brother-in-law, whose name is Paul. These two grown men rose above me and knew that a human life is murder. They weren't fighting about Paul's love for my sister. They were fighting with each other because one strong man, a factory worker, was laid off from his work, and the other strong man, the driver of a coal truck, was laid off from his work. They were both determined to live their lives, and so they glared at each other and said they were going to live, come hell or high water. High water is not trite in southern Ohio. Nothing is trite along a river. My father died a good death. To die a good death means to live one's life. I don't say a good life.

I say a life.

## Beautiful Ohio

Those old Winnebago men
Knew what they were singing.
All summer long and all alone,
I had found a way
To sit on a railroad tie
Above the sewer main.
It spilled a shining waterfall out of a pipe
Somebody had gouged through the slanted earth.
Sixteen thousand and five hundred more or less people
In Martins Ferry, my home, my native country,
Quickened the river
With the speed of light.
And the light caught there
The solid speed of their lives
In the instant of that waterfall.
I know what we call it
Most of the time.
But I have my own song for it,
And sometimes, even today,
I call it beauty.

# Miners Shaking Hands with a Union Man

from a photograph

These men are solemn and strong,
their lungs black and bituminous.
Behind the photographer, Peabody's goons.

The woman, half-visible on the fringe
of the vignette, feels that way:
her husband vanished in the dark snow of a cave in.

And closely, through the heavy grain,
you can see they are armed.
The blunt handle of a shovel curled

in an arm's crook, a chain
wrapped around a fist
like a large and fraternal ring.

This is a show of force: it is not
important that the pale-skinned Peabody men
sweat around the butts of revolvers,

but that they know for once
the isolation of the mines,
the impenetrable blackness off camera.

# Diary of the Strike

### May 21, 1939

Picket lines are for fingers and legs:
how thin they are, how easy they'd give
under axe handles.
                        At noon
The Union Rep comes with a bag of radishes
and rye bread. We give thanks
for our fortunes: Billy Carruthers ran
the length of Mascoutah, Illinois
with his ankle bones chiseled off
and two nickels ringing in his pocket:
he could have lost it all.

The strikebreakers, cleaning their teeth
near the pool hall, are rumored to spit-
shine their boots with miners' blood.

When my line duty's over I'll get
right home. Potatoes and cabbage for dinner
again, but who'd complain? The goons
slice their steaks with the same knives
that cut off noses and thumbs. Near dark
we're all thumbs: the placards shaking,
the alleys lit with shadows.
                        No one's afraid
really. Just hungry, looking forward to dinner,
walking quietly home.

## From Lumaghi Mine

Dear Father,
                    Eleven days without sunlight. We go in
in the black morning fog, work and come out
having missed it all. We begin to appreciate the dark.
Too bright outside: faces white
as carbide, the shrill discs of real dishes.
It takes two days to get used to peripheral vision
again, the head light without the lamp.
    We rest after loading each car.
In that silence the seeping gas trickles,
as if we fished an underground stream for hours
without hearing water. So pain comes too,
when the muscles are still.

    I write while the others sleep. By the light
of my headgear the pencil feels like a pickaxe.
The moon is my sun and the sculptures
on the mine walls shimmer into constellations.
I have learned how not to see.

    Sometimes I am shocked by the whiteness
of my cuticles, glowing out of the nails
like slivers from an eclipse. They bob across the page,
fireflies, men walking up a shaft with lit lamps.
And the worn shovels, the hands, hang alongside
the body, coal dust healed into the calluses.
They seem odd, astir in the milk of the bedclothes
like frail and discolored spoons.

    Father, we are all the same. Dust fills in
the oldest wrinkles, the deepest scars. You see,
I am blackening: grey knuckles,
ears silting over. My eyes
are black as anthracite. The sun could ignite them
and they would burn for days.

## Oh Yeah, the Mine Talks

                              Secrets
ain't no part of it though, just good learnin'.
And you better pay attention. When them timbers
creak just so it means they're givin' up
and lettin' down—sorta like bones,
the way a knee pops a little too loud
one last time. You smack the roof
of the loadin' room a few times
with the handle of your shovel before steppin' in.
Coal up there's supposed to sound good,
*thunka thunka* like a ripe melon. If it don't,
if it sounds muddy or don't ring even a little,
she's gonna fall. Maybe right then.
You gotta move fast. Then
there's the sounds a miner can't hear.
Too high, a dog whistle, a train way outa town.
Watch: cause rats hear it. A little
hiss of gas comin' in. That's when you wish.
All that time cussin' them rats for stealin'
your sandwich, laughin' about the one
what stole Henry's false teeth, or them whiskers
drug across your ankles that made your bones go cold:
you wish they was all here. But those rats,
they gone. Crawled out through their holes.
And you ain't never leavin' yours.

JAMES B. ALLEN grew up on a farm in the Midwest and worked in a brass factory to earn money for college. His books are *Beggars Could Ride* and *See the Lighthouse Burning*.

CATHERINE ANDERSON teaches writing and English as a second language to Spanish-speaking women in the Boston area. Her collection of poems is *In the Mother Tongue*.

MAGGIE ANDERSON was born in New York City and spent her teenage years in West Virginia, where she discovered her family's Appalachian heritage. Her books are *Years That Answer* and *Cold Comfort*.

ANTLER has worked as a dishwasher, gas pumper, encyclopedia salesman, and house painter and has done factory work at Harley Davidson and Continental Can Company. His books are *Factory* and *Last Words*.

RICHARD BLESSING, now deceased, grew up in northwestern Pennsylvania and taught for many years at the University of Washington. His poetry is collected in *A Closed Book* and *Winter Constellations*.

ROBERT BLY writes, "I come from farmers in Norway who moved to this country in 1855 and my father was a farmer in western Minnesota. I grew up doing farm work." His 1967 book, *The Light around the Body*, won the National Book Award. *Selected Poems* appeared in 1986.

DEBORAH BOE lives in Boston. Her first collection of poems is *Mojave*.

JOSEPH BRUCHAC worked as a laborer, surveyor, and tree surgeon during his school years, and also taught English and literature in West Africa from 1966 to 1969. *Near the Mountains: New and Selected Poems* was published in 1987.

DAVID BUDBILL has worked as a short-order cook, gardener, carpenter's apprentice, and English teacher. His four poetry collections are *Pulp Cutters' Nativity, From Down to the Village, The Chain Saw Dance,* and *Why I Came to Judevine*. He lives in the remote mountains of northern Vermont.

LORNA DEE CERVANTES is a Chicana poet now living in Colorado. Her first book, *Emplumada,* explores the themes of identity, domestic violence, and social oppression from a feminist viewpoint.

DAVID CITINO teaches at the Ohio State University. His books are *The Gift of Fire* and *The Appassionata Doctrines.*

MARY JOAN COLEMAN is a West Virginia poet. Her first collection is *Take One Blood Red Rose.*

NICHOLAS COLES teaches and writes about working-class literature and reading poetry at the University of Pittsburgh, where he also directs the Western Pennsylvania Writing Project.

BRENDA CONNOR-BEY is a member of the Harlem Writers Guild. Her poems have appeared in a number of anthologies, including *Confirmation* and *Black & in Brooklyn.*

VICTOR CONTOSKI teaches at the University of Kansas. His books include *A Kansas Sequence* and *Names.*

JIM DANIELS grew up in a working-class neighborhood in Detroit and worked summers in a Ford axle plant to earn money for college. His book *Places / Everyone* won the 1985 Brittingham Prize in Poetry. *Punching Out* is his most recent collection.

KATE DANIELS teaches writing at Louisiana State University. Her books of poetry are *The White Wave,* winner of the 1983 Agnes Lynch Starrett Prize, and *The Niobe Poems.* She is the co-editor of *Poetry East.*

JAMES DEN BOER is the author of *Lost in Blue Canyon, Nine Poems,* and other books. He lives in California.

PATRICIA DOBLER was born and raised in Middletown, Ohio, a small steel town. Her first collection of poems, *Talking to Strangers,* won the 1986 Brittingham Prize in Poetry. She lives in Pittsburgh.

STEPHEN DUNN is the author of several books, including *Between Angels, Local Time, Not Dancing,* and *Work and Love.* He lives in Port Republic, New Jersey.

HARLEY ELLIOTT teaches art at Marymount College of Kansas, in Salina. His books of poetry include *The Citizen Game* and *Darkness at Each Elbow.*

MARY FELL worked for several years as a social worker and now teaches English at Indiana University's East Campus in Richmond. Her book

*The Persistence of Memory* was a selection of the 1984 National Poetry Series.

ERICA FUNKHOUSER lives in Essex, Massachusetts. Her poetry has appeared in *Poetry, Ploughshares,* and *The Paris Review.* Her first book is *Natural Affinities.*

TESS GALLAGHER grew up in the logging camps of the Pacific Northwest near Port Angeles, Washington. She teaches in the writing program at Syracuse University. Her books of poetry include *Amplitude, Willingly, Under Stars,* and *Instructions to the Double.*

BRENDAN GALVIN lives in Durham, Connecticut. His books of poetry include *Wampanoag Traveler, Seals in the Inner Harbor, Winter Oysters,* and *Great Blue.*

GARY GILDNER lives in Des Moines, Iowa. His most recent book of poetry is *Blue Like the Heavens.*

JOHN GIORNO is a New York City performance poet. His most recent book is *Grasping at Emptiness.*

ALICE WIRTH GRAY lives in Berkeley, California. Her poems have appeared in *Poetry, The American Scholar,* and other magazines.

DONALD HALL taught English at the University of Michigan from 1957 until 1975; since then he has been a free-lance writer. In 1988 his book *The One Day* won the National Book Critics Circle Award in poetry. He lives in New Hampshire.

C. G. HANZLICEK teaches at California State University, Fresno. His books include *When There Are No Secrets* and *Calling the Dead.*

GWEN HAUSER has worked various jobs including factory work, waitressing, mail sorting, and modeling for art classes. Among her recent books is *The Ordinary Invisible Woman.*

EDWARD HIRSCH teaches at the University of Houston. His first book of poems, *For the Sleepwalkers,* won the Delmore Schwartz Memorial Award. His most recent book is *The Night Parade.*

JONATHAN HOLDEN teaches at Kansas State University. His books of poetry include *The Names of the Rapids, Falling from Stardom,* and *Leverage.*

RICHARD HUGO (1923–82) grew up in Seattle, served as a bombardier during World War II, and worked for Boeing for twelve years before beginning a teaching career at the University of Montana. *Making*

*Certain It Goes On: The Collected Poems of Richard Hugo* was published in 1984.

DAVID IGNATOW grew up in Brooklyn, the son of a Russian immigrant skilled in the art of bookbinding. He worked in his father's bindery and as a shipyard handyman, public relations writer, salesman, and eventually as treasurer and president of a bindery firm. He is the author of *Leaving the Door Open, Whisper to the Earth,* and many other books.

TODD JAILER worked for five years for an electric utility in Pittsburgh and is now a member of the South End Press publishing collective in Boston. His book *Power and Light* is forthcoming from Curbstone Press.

JUNE JORDAN is the author of *Civil Wars, Living Room, On Call,* and many other books. She teaches at SUNY, Stony Brook.

LAWRENCE JOSEPH grew up in Detroit, worked for a time in the auto plants there, and now works as a lawyer and teaches law at St. Johns University. His books are *Shouting at No One,* winner of the 1982 Agnes Lynch Starrett Prize, and *Curriculum Vitae.*

LAWRENCE KEARNEY was born in Oxford, England, and grew up in Buffalo, New York. His first collection of poems is *Kingdom Come.*

EDWARD T. LAHEY, now deceased, wrote about the life and work of miners and was a frequent contributor to *Poetry Northwest.*

MIRIAM LEVINE is the author of *The Graves of Delawanna* and *To Know We Are Living.* She lives in Arlington, Massachusetts.

PHILIP LEVINE grew up in Detroit, where he worked a variety of jobs that entailed heavy labor, including work in the auto factories. His most recent books of poetry are *A Walk with Tom Jefferson, Sweet Will,* and *Selected Poems.*

CHRIS LLEWELLYN is a self-described labor poet. Her book *Fragments from the Fire: The Triangle Shirtwaist Company Fire of March 25, 1911* won the 1986 Walt Whitman Award of the American Academy of Poets.

ROBERT LOUTHAN lives in Cambridge, Massachusetts. His books of poetry are *Living in Code* and *Shrunken Planets.*

CHARLES CASEY MARTIN is a contributor to *Poetry Northwest* and other magazines.

SUZANNE MATSON teaches at Boston College. Her poetry has appeared in *American Poetry Review, Poetry,* and *Poetry Northwest.*

ROBERT MEZEY teaches at Pomona College in Claremont, California. His most recent poetry collection is *Evening Wind.*

LISEL MUELLER lives in Lake Forest, Illinois. Her most recent books are *The Need to Hold Still* and *Second Language.*

JOYCE CAROL OATES grew up in the countryside north of Buffalo in a working-class household, her father a member of the United Auto Workers. She teaches at Princeton University and is the author of many books of fiction, poetry, and prose.

ED OCHESTER is the director of the Writing Program at the University of Pittsburgh and the editor of the Pitt Poetry Series, published by the University of Pittsburgh Press. His books of poetry include *Changing the Name to Ochester, Miracle Mile,* and *Dancing on the Edges of Knives.*

MICHAEL O'CONNOR grew up a steelworker's son in the mill town of Carnegie, Pennsylvania. His poems have appeared in *The Minnesota Review* and other magazines.

PETER ORESICK grew up in Ford City, Pennsylvania, a mill town north of Pittsburgh, and worked summers in a glass factory to earn money for college. His poetry collections are *An American Peace, Other Lives, The Story of Glass,* and *Definitions.*

GREG PAPE lives in Stevensville, Montana. His poetry collections are *Border Crossings* and *Black Branches.*

JAY PARINI, a poet and novelist, teaches English at Middlebury College in Vermont. His books of poetry include *Anthracite Country* and *Town Life.*

KENNETH PATCHEN (1911–72) was born in Niles, Ohio. He authored many books of poetry, which are represented in *The Collected Poems of Kenneth Patchen.*

DONALD A. PETESCH worked on the assembly line at a Fischer Body plant in Oakland, California, and now teaches at the University of Pittsburgh. His poems have appeared in *Poetry Northwest, Southern Poetry Review,* and other magazines.

ANTHONY PETROSKY grew up in the anthracite coal region of northeastern Pennsylvania. His first collection of poems, *Jurgis Petraskas,* won the 1982 Walt Whitman Award of the Academy of American Poets. He teaches at the University of Pittsburgh.

KEVIN RIPPIN grew up in Johnstown, Pennsylvania, the son of a steelworker, and has worked as a public relations writer. His book is *One Shuddering Tremolo.*

DAVID RIVARD grew up in the New England mill town of Fall River, Massachusetts. His first book, *Torque,* won the 1987 Agnes Lynch Starrett Poetry Prize.

LEN ROBERTS grew up in Cohoes, New York, a small textile town. His books include *Black Wings* and *Sweet Ones.*

CAROLYN M. RODGERS lives in Oakland, California. Her books of poetry include *Morning Glory, Adobe,* and *A Little Lower Than the Angels.*

LIZ ROSENBERG teaches at SUNY, Binghamton. Her first book, *The Fire Music,* won the 1985 Agnes Lynch Starrett Poetry Prize.

VERN RUTSALA lives in Portland, Oregon. His books include *Ruined Cities, Backtracking,* and *Walking Home from the Ice-House.*

MICHAEL RYAN lives in Charlottesville, Virginia. His first volume of poetry, *Threats Instead of Trees,* won the Yale Series of Younger Poets Award. His other books are *In Winter* and *God Hunger.*

JAMES SCULLY, a poet and social activist, lives in Willimantic, Connecticut. His books of poetry include *Apollo Helmet, Santiago Poems,* and *May Day.*

GARY SOTO teaches at the University of California, Berkeley. His books of poetry are *Black Hair, Where Sparrows Work Hard, The Tale of Sunlight,* and *The Elements of San Joaquin.*

SUSAN STEWART teaches at Temple University. Her first poetry collection is *Yellow Stars and Ice.*

CONSTANCE URDANG lives in St. Louis. Her books of poetry include *The Lone Woman and Others* and *Only the World.*

DAVID WAGONER is the author of many books of poetry, most recently *First Light* and *Through the Forest.* He lives in Mill Creek, Washington.

RONALD WALLACE directs the Creative Writing Program at the University of Wisconsin, Madison. His poetry collections are *People and Dog in the Sun* and *Tunes for Bears to Dance To.*

Tom Wayman has worked various jobs including college teaching, construction, and assemblyman in a truck factory. He has published several collections of poetry and has edited two anthologies of mostly Canadian work poems, *Going for Coffee* and *A Government Job at Last*.

Robert Winner, now deceased, worked for many years in the financial industry on Wall Street. *Flogging the Czar* and *Green in the Body* are two of his published volumes.

Andrew Wreggitt has published poetry, short fiction, and nonfiction in many magazines. He is the author of *Riding through Nicola Country*.

James Wright (1927–80) was born in Martins Ferry, Ohio, a mill town on the banks of the Ohio River, the son of a glassworker. Among his many books are *This Journey, To a Blossoming Pear Tree,* and *Collected Poems*.

Robert Wrigley teaches English at Lewis-Clark State College in Idaho. His poetry collections are *Moon in a Mason Jar, The Glow,* and *The Sinking of Clay City*.

# SUBJECT INDEX

263